P9-AGN-191

HERCULES

WITHDRAWN

Extraordinary Jobs in

ENTERTAINMENT

Also in the Extraordinary Jobs series:

Extraordinary Jobs in

ENTERTAINMENT

ALECIA T. DEVANTIER & CAROL A. TURKINGTON

Ferguson
An imprint of Infobase Publishing

CONTRA COSTA COUNTY LIBRARY

3 1901 04079 4291

Extraordinary Jobs in Entertainment

Copyright © 2006 by Alecia T. Devantier and Carol A. Turkington

All rights reserved. No part of this book may be reproduced or utilized in any form or by any means, electronic or mechanical, including photocopying, recording, or by any information storage or retrieval systems, without permission in writing from the publisher. For information contact:

Ferguson
An imprint of Infobase Publishing
132 West 31st Street
New York NY 10001

Library of Congress Cataloging-in-Publication Data

Devantier, Alecia T.
  Extraordinary jobs in entertainment / Alecia T. Devantier and Carol A. Turkington.
    p. cm.
  ISBN 0-8160-5855-5 (hc : alk. paper)
  Includes bibliographical references and index.
  1. Performing arts—Vocational guidance. I. Turkington, Carol. II. Title.
  PN1580.D48 2006
791'.023—dc22   2005024485

Ferguson books are available at special discounts when purchased in bulk quantities for businesses, associations, institutions, or sales promotions. Please call our Special Sales Department in New York at (212) 967-8800 or (800) 322-8755.

You can find Ferguson on the World Wide Web at http://www.fergpubco.com

Text design by Mary Susan Ryan-Flynn
Cover design by Salvatore Luongo

Printed in the United States of America

VB KT 10 9 8 7 6 5 4 3 2 1

This book is printed on acid-free paper.

CONTENTS

ACKNOWLEDGMENTS

This book wouldn't have been possible without the help of countless others who referred us to individuals to interview and who came up with information about a wide variety of odd and unusual jobs. We deeply appreciate the time and generosity of all those individuals who took the time to talk to us about their unusual jobs in the entertainment business. Thanks also to all the people who helped with interviews and information and the production of this book, including Susan Shelly McGovern.

Thanks also to our editors James Chambers and Sarah Fogarty, to Vanessa Nittoli, and to our agents Ed Claflin of Ed Claflin Literary Associates and Gene Brissie.

ARE YOU CUT OUT FOR A CAREER IN ENTERTAINMENT?

Would you rather jump out of a speeding car at 90 miles an hour than work underneath one? Would you rather dangle a boom mike than a fishing line? Do you dream of singing opera, dancing a ballet, or dashing off designs on a storyboard—or are you solely focused on getting out that company annual report? Would you find it exciting to tag along on a film shoot in the Kalahari Desert in the middle of summer as a set medic—or would you rather tend scrapes and cuts in the local elementary school?

Let's face it: Most people in the entertainment industry not only step to the beat of a different drummer—they may well be part of the band. They're made for long hours, hard work, and all sorts of unusual talents. You might find them jumping out of a plane, getting up at 3 a.m. to get a movie star a quart of Chunky Monkey ice cream, or building an entire miniature city in the middle of nowhere out of cardboard and paste. One thing's for sure: They'll never fit inside a normal 9-to-5 time slot.

And that's okay.

Take some time to think about the kind of person you are, and the sorts of experiences you dream of having. Ask yourself: *Is there something I'd rather be doing for the rest of my life that would make me truly happy? Am I passionate about something?*

If you want a career in entertainment, you'd better be passionate, because this is a job path with incredible competition, long hours, hard knocks, and heartbreak. But if you manage, somehow, to get your toe in the door—maybe your uncle's aunt's son Warren knows the next-door neighbor of the producer—there's a tantalizing payoff. Almost everyone in the entertainment world *loves* what they do.

Of course, if it's the bright lights of actual stardom you're pining for, realize that only a very, very small minority ever gets the chance for incredible success—the kind of success that brings huge salaries, perks, and recognition. For every star, there are 2,000 wannabes who didn't make the cut. But most of them don't have regrets, because for these people, the payoff was in the attempt, not the arrival.

But there's another way to reach for that golden ring called *Hollywood*. You don't have to work in front of the cameras to get a taste of the glitz and glamour. If you dream of working in the entertainment business but you turn pale at the thought of getting up in front of a crowd, you might consider becoming a gaffer, a best boy, or a focus puller, where you'll be working behind the camera. Do you want to contribute to the industry in a different way? Study entertainment sales or marketing. Or you could become a producer or director! There are all sorts of interesting, unusual jobs behind the scenes in entertainment that require just as much talent and dedication. Working in the entertainment field in any of these jobs can be an incredible experience that will let your spirit soar, and allow you to do what you love.

Of course, loving what you do is only part of having a successful career in entertainment. You have to be willing to work hard. Too often kids have the idea that they'll graduate into a world of theater, movies, films, TV, radio, or stand-up with people just dying to give them a job.

It may not always be easy. It can be unbelievably hard to get started in entertainment, because most jobs in this business are union controlled. To get a job, you've got to join the union. But to join the union, you've got to have experience. Luckily there is some nonunion work to be had in the field, giving beginners the experience they need to get started.

Of course, a lucky few are born into entertainment families, where Mom or Dad or Aunt Kara already works in the business, and *voila!* You've inherited a career. The rest of you may just have inherited a lot of *shoulds*. These *shoulds* inside your head can be a major stumbling block in finding and enjoying an unusual career in entertainment.

Everybody knows about the typical jobs that are out there. We wrote this book to help you see the world of unusual careers you may never have thought about—jobs you may not have known existed, or that you didn't realize paid a decent salary. Once you see the possibilities, start dreaming about how to reach them. Remember, if you've got a dream, you owe it to yourself to go after it, no matter how unusual or difficult or just plain batty it may seem to others.

You'll need to realize that there may be other people who aren't so happy with your career choice. You may hear complaints from your family and friends who just can't understand why you don't want a "regular" job. Some people think working in entertainment only qualifies as a hobby—something you do until a "real" job comes along. They may tell you: "Surely you don't intend to make a living getting up on stage and telling jokes!" If you confide your career dreams to some of these people, you may find they try to discourage you. Can you handle their continuous skepticism?

Don't cheat yourself. If you don't do what you were born to do—well, you're going to get older anyway. You might as well get older doing what you love to do… what you *need* to do.

What became clear as we researched this book is that a career in entertainment is more than a job—it's a way of looking at life, with gusto and verve. Living and working in the entertainment business isn't necessarily an easy career. But if you allow yourself to explore the options that are out there, you'll find that work and play often tend to become the same thing. So push past your doubts and fears—and let your journey begin!

Carol A. Turkington
Alecia T. Devantier

HOW TO USE THIS BOOK

Students face a lot of pressure to decide what they want to be when they grow up. If you're not interested in a traditional 9-to-5 job—maybe you're the artsy theatrical type who loves to entertain or the techno sort who loves fiddling with recording equipment—you're probably looking for a unique way to make a living. But where can you go to get answers to your questions about these exciting, creative, nontraditional jobs?

Where can you go to find out how to become a focus puller? Do you have what it takes to become a director of photography? Where do you learn how to be a gaffer or a grip? Is it really possible to make a living as a set medic? Where would you go for training if you wanted to be a product placement specialist? What's the job outlook for a conductor?

Look no further! This book will take you inside the world of a number of different occupations in the field of entertainment, answering your questions, letting you know what to expect if you pursue that career, introducing you to someone making a living that way, and providing resources if you want to do further research.

THE JOB PROFILES

All job profiles in this book have been broken down into the following fact-filled sections: At a Glance, Overview, and Interview. Each offers a distinct perspective on the job, and taken together give you a full view of the job in question.

At a Glance

Each profile starts out with an At a Glance box, offering a snapshot of important basic information to give you a quick glimpse of that particular job, including salary, education/experience, personal attributes, requirements, and outlook.

✅ *Salary range.* What can you expect to make? Salary ranges for the jobs in this book are as accurate as possible; many are based on data from the U.S. Bureau of Labor Statistics' *Occupational Outlook Handbook*. Information also comes from individuals, actual job ads, employers, and experts in that field. It's important to remember that especially in the entertainment industry, salaries for any particular job vary greatly depending on your experience, geographic location, and your past history. For example, a summer stock actor playing Macbeth on Cape Cod could not hope to earn what a major star on Broadway would bring portraying the same Danish prince. The difference isn't in the play—it's the performer, the location, and the other cast members.

✅ *Education/Experience.* What kind of education or experience does the job require? This section will give you some information about the types of education requirements that jobs in the entertainment field might have.

For some jobs on stage, education isn't nearly as important as experience, but for more technical positions, a solid education in electronics or production is required. Many entertainment positions are union jobs, which means you'll have to jump through an extra set of hoops on your way to making your dream come true.

✔ *Personal attributes.* Do you have what it takes to do this job? How do you think of yourself? How would someone else describe you? This section will give you an idea of some of the personality traits that might be useful in this career. These attributes were collected from articles written about the jobs, as well as recommendations from employers and people actually doing the jobs, working in the field.

✔ *Requirements.* Are you qualified? Some jobs have strict requirements or union membership rules; more technical jobs may require certification or licensure. You might as well make sure you meet any health, medical, or screening requirements before going any further with your job pursuit.

✔ *Outlook.* What are your chances of finding a job? This section is based in part on the *Occupational Outlook Handbook*, as well as interviews with employers and experts doing the jobs. This information is typically a best guess based on the information that is available right now, including changes in the economy, situations in the country, and job trends, as well as many other factors that can influence changes in the availability of these and other jobs.

Overview

This section will really give you an idea of what to expect from the job. For most of these jobs in the entertainment field, there really is no such thing as an average day. Each new day, new job, or new assignment is a whole new adventure, bringing with it a unique set of challenges and rewards. This section provides an overview of what a person holding this position might expect on a day-to-day basis.

This section also gives more details about how to get into the profession. It takes a more detailed look at the required training or education, if needed, giving an in-depth look at what to expect during that training or educational period. If there are no training or education requirements for the job, this section will provide some suggestions for getting the experience you'll need to be successful.

No job is perfect, and **Pitfalls** takes a look at some of the obvious and not-so-obvious pitfalls of the job. Don't let the pitfalls discourage you from pursuing the career; they are just things to be aware of while making your decision.

For many people, loving your job so much that you look forward to going to work every day is enough of a perk. **Perks** will look at some of the other perks of the job you may not have considered.

So what can you do *now* to start working toward the career of your dreams? **Get a Jump on the Job** will give you some ideas and suggestions for things that you can do now, even before graduating, to start preparing for this job. Opportunities include courses you can take now in high school that will help you later; training programs, groups and organizations to join, as well as practical skills to learn.

Interview

In addition to taking a general look at the job, each profile features a discussion with someone who is lucky enough to do this job for a living. In addition to giving you an inside look at the job, the experts offer advice for people wanting to follow in their footsteps, pursuing a career in the same field.

APPENDIXES

Appendix A (Associations, Organizations, and Web Sites) lists places to look for additional information about each specific job, including professional associations, societies, unions, government organizations, Web sites, and periodicals. Associations and other groups are a great source of information, and there's an association for just about every job you can imagine. Many groups and associations have a student membership level, which you can join by paying a small fee. There are many advantages to joining an association, including the chance to make important contacts, receive helpful newsletters, and attend workshops or conferences. Some associations also offer scholarships that will make it easier to further your education.

Other sources listed in this section include information about accredited training programs, forums, and more. All of this information is current as of the writing of this book, but Web site addresses do change. If you can't find what you're looking for at a given address, do a simple search—the page may have been moved to a different location.

In **Appendix B (Online Career Resources)** we've gathered some of the best general Web sites about unusual jobs in the field of entertainment. Use these as a springboard to your own Internet research. All of this information was current as this book was written, but Web site addresses do change. If you can't find what you're looking for at a given address, do a simple Web search—the page may have been moved to a different location.

Appendix C (Film Schools) lists some of the best places to study theater, film, and production.

READ MORE ABOUT IT

In this back-of-the-book listing, we've gathered some helpful books that can give you more detailed information about each job we discuss in this book. Find these at the library or bookstore if you want to learn even more about entertainment jobs.

ANIMAL WRANGLER

OVERVIEW

If Lassie needs to run to a well to pull Timmy out of harm's way, you can bet there was an animal trainer behind the trick. When Eddie, the bouncy dog on TV's *Frasier*, leaps into action, you just know an animal trainer is lurking just off set, giving directions.

Animals have appeared in movies, television shows, and commercials for almost as long as there have been movies and TV shows and commercials. *White Fang*, *Lassie*, *The Whale Rider*, *Mr. Ed*, *The Horse Whisperer*, *Frasier*, *Secondhand Lions*, *Snow Dogs*, and *Homeward Bound* are just a few examples of movies and TV shows throughout the years that have featured trained animals. Animals also have been trained to star in TV commercials and appear in print advertisements.

We all know that animals aren't born knowing how to open doors, pull sleds in formation, or carry humans on their backs. So, how is it that there are tigers and bears who can pretend that they're attacking people, elephants who are happy to carry people in their trunks, or birds who'll swoop down and pick up an object on command and they fly away again?

These animals are painstakingly trained by professional animal trainers, who might spend months teaching an animal to do a particular stunt. Animals can be taught to do amazing things, but the trainer must be able to determine which animals possess the ability and aptitude

AT A GLANCE

Salary Range

The average national salary for animal wranglers in the entertainment biz ranges from about $17,000 to $24,000 a year, according to government statistics. Earnings depend on the types of animals involved, the person's experience level, and the location. Wranglers in demand within the entertainment industry can make much more than the national average.

Education/Experience

While there are no formal educational requirements for animal wranglers, a degree in an area such as animal management, marine biology, animal science, zoology, or a related field is recommended.

Personal Attributes

You should have a great degree of patience, because training animals can be slow and frustrating. In addition to skill in communicating with animals, you'll also need to be able to communicate with other people in order to exchange ideas and concepts with producers, production designers, and other clients. Ideally, you'll be in good physical condition since training animals can be physically strenuous.

Requirements

You won't succeed if you don't have a genuine love and admiration for animals. Some states require animal trainers to be licensed or certified.

Outlook

Animal trainer jobs are expected to increase by between 10 and 20 percent through the year 2012. That job growth is considered to be average. However, there are very few animal trainers in the industry, so the increase doesn't reflect a large jump in numbers.

for training, and be willing to put in the time and effort to make it happen.

The job of a wrangler is to teach animals to perform tricks, obey commands quickly, and be comfortable in different situations. In the 2005 movie *Because of Winn-Dixie*, the dogs (there were five of them) were taught to howl, sneeze, and shake their heads on cue. Before that could happen, however, the animal trainer spent about eight weeks just teaching the dogs basic skills and making sure they'd be comfortable in many different situations.

Professionals who train animals for movies and television usually have their own supply of animals obtained in a variety of ways. For example, a professional wrangler may have a business partner who scouts for likely animals who might make good movie stars. The *Because of Winn-Dixie* dogs, for instance, were finally located in France after months of searching.

Once a wrangler has a group of well-trained animals, he or she may send the animal out on an audition for a part, or a director or production designer may contact the trainer to arrange for required

Connie Rusgen, entertainment animal wrangler

Connie Rusgen has taught rats to run mazes and pigeons to land on an actor's shoulder, remain there until the actor finished talking, and then fly off in a specific direction. She's trained dogs and cats that have appeared in such movies as *Catwoman, The Karate Dogs, Air Bud: Spikes Back, Cats & Dogs, Best In Show,* and *Mermaid*. She also works with parrots, cats, and mice. In short, Connie Rusgen loves animals, and she's been able to make a career out of training them for film and TV.

However, the work isn't easy for this Vancouver animal trainer, who spends long hours working with and worrying about the collection of beasts she owns. In addition to training, she transports them to auditions and shoot sites for films and TV shows, monitors their progress, and looks out for their well-being.

A typical day for Rusgen begins early in the morning, when she cleans the animals and their quarters, gives them all fresh water, and makes sure each gets some exercise. When those daily chores are finished, she begins planning her training strategy for the day, choosing the animal or animals she'll be working with and the behaviors that she needs to address. She'll decide what she hopes to accomplish and then she prepares the treats she uses as incentives.

Rusgen's strategy is to not tire or frustrate any animal, so she works in short sessions, allowing the animal to rest in between. "I must always end the session on a positive note and leave the animal eager to do more," Rusgen says. "While one animal is on break, I can stay busy by working with another one."

Her favorite part of her job, Rusgen says, is when an animal finally responds to her training and performs in the manner she was hoping. While the actual training is a joy for Rusgen, she finds parts of the job tedious. She must carefully track and record the progress of each animal and keep track of its preferred diet, monitor what it eats on a daily basis, and record its weight, daily habits, and so forth. Any animals that travel or are insured need to have health certificates and proofs of vaccinations.

She keeps a close eye on her animals, watching for the smallest signs of sickness or other trouble. Her job, Rusgen says, is to keep the animals not only healthy, but happy, as well.

animals. But while it may sound like a lot of fun, training animals for movies and television shows and commercials involves a great deal of work. Training is the fun part—but unless you have help, working with animals also means hours spent cleaning pens, stalls, kennels, and yards; feeding; and exercising.

Pitfalls

Training animals is difficult, and many people who try it find they don't have the tremendous amount of patience required for the job. Because there are relatively few jobs for animals in the entertainment industry, most of them are given to well established, experienced trainers who have connections to directors and production designers. It's a difficult field to break into.

Perks

If you want to be a part of the entertainment industry and you really love working with animals, what could be a better job

She got her start with animals when she volunteered at her local animal shelter as a teenager. A bit later she worked in a dog grooming shop and volunteered to clean pens and cages at the nearby zoo, experience that she considers to be invaluable. "It's very, very important to learn about animals from the beginning by cleaning cages," Rusgen says. "You learn to look for signs of ill health or behavior problems."

Determined to learn all that she could about dogs, which were her focus during her teens and early 20s, Rusgen took several dog training and behavior classes, attended seminars, and read everything she could find about training dogs. When her interest broadened to include other animals, she started learning everything that she could about cats, birds, and rodents. "I wanted that challenge of working with them all," Rusgen says. "I wanted to understand how they thought and what their motivations were."

Her love of training animals has increased over the years, and she continues to enjoy the challenge of getting animals to perform in movies and on TV. Rusgen works with two partners, both of whom have large dogs that they and Rusgen train. One of the partners also manages the business end of the operation. "There are lots of other animals required in film besides just dogs, but dogs are the bread and butter for any trainer," Rusgen says. "Dogs work more often and more regularly."

Rusgen suggests that if you're interested in becoming a professional animal trainer, you should start working at an animal shelter, kennel, or stable, where you'll learn valuable tips. If there's a training facility in your area, it would be a good idea to volunteer there and observe how actual training is done.

If you have a pet, you can get a good head start by training the animal and then showing the results to a professional trainer. The trainer is likely to be impressed that you've taken the time and initiative to work on your own, and it will give you a feeling for how far you and your pet have advanced.

than training dogs, horses, lions, birds, porcupines, or other animals to perform in movies or on TV shows? You not only get to spend a lot of time with animals, you also get to hang out with show-biz types, and travel to exotic places to film. And an experienced, connected entertainment animal trainer can command a large salary.

Get a Jump on the Job

Volunteer or get a job in a shelter, kennel, or stable and pay close attention to every facet of animal care. Notice their different personalities, what they eat, which ones seem cooperative and open to training, and which ones are more aloof. Get to know the signs of sickness, and learn everything you can about the animals and their care. If you have a dog, you could enroll in a dog training or dog agility course. If you don't have a dog, offer to take a friend's dog. Read all the books you can find about training animals and visit the Web sites of animal trainers to get tips and learn more about the business.

BEST BOY

OVERVIEW

Best boy is a curious name for a job that's really more like an assistant. A best boy is the second in command to a *gaffer*, the lighting electrician on a movie set. Still, the job of best boy is important in a filming situation, and qualified, experienced best boys are held in high regard. Together with the lighting electrician, a best boy must be able to figure out how to set up lights to create a particular type of lighting and find a way to successfully power the lights.

Basically, a best boy does anything that the gaffer asks him to. He (or she—there also are best girls) helps with moving, setting up, and taking down lighting equipment; works with the gaffer to figure out power sources for all of the equipment; makes suggestions to the gaffer concerning the placement of lights; climbs ladders to install lighting fixtures; and so on.

While the best boy is second in line to the gaffer, he normally is in charge of delegating other workers to unload equipment from trucks and get it set up according to the lighting plan that's been established.

Obviously, lighting is very important to a production, whether it's a film, TV show, commercial, live theater, or video. Best boys must help gaffers to create moods with lighting. For example, when you see a beautiful sunset in a commercial, that sunset was generated by a particular color of plastic sheeting (called a *gel*) installed over a light. Did you ever see a subway scene in which the train lights flickered, or watch a shadow move across the screen, or

AT A GLANCE

Salary Range

Salaries for best boys vary widely, depending on the employer, circumstances of employment, and availability of jobs. Best boys may be paid by the project or on a daily or hourly basis. The average yearly salary for a best boy ranges from $23,000 to $44,000 a year.

Education/Experience

While there are no specific educational requirements to be a best boy, many employers will prefer that you have a degree in an area such as theater arts or entertainment technology. You'll need to have electrical training, so you might consider a high school vocational program, or pursue a degree from a community college or technical school. Some schools have programs specific to film production and technical lighting.

Personal Attributes

Should have good communications skills and be able to grasp ideas quickly. Must be willing to follow instructions and work as part of a team, and be willing to work long hours. It takes a lot of drive and ambition to succeed in almost any area of the entertainment industry, including that of best boy.

Requirements

You must be qualified as an electrician, and have experience working with electrical systems. Certification may be required. Some employers may require experience as a junior electrician before considering you for best boy, and others may require membership in a union.

Outlook

Jobs as a best boy are expected to increase by between 10 and 20 percent through the year 2012, according to government figures. That job growth is considered to be average.

notice car lights flash against a wall? Those are all lighting tricks, and it's up to the best

Dennis Haden, best boy

Dennis Haden is technically called a freelance technician, but many of his jobs have been that of best boy. With a dual degree in radio, TV, and film and in art photography from North Texas State University, Haden has gained a vast amount of valuable working experience since starting out in business in 1985. He's worked on many motion pictures, national and regional commercials, and music videos for the biggest artists in country music, rap, rhythm and blues, and rock.

On a typical day as a best boy, Haden gets the equipment trucks to the set, and figures out how close he'll be able to park them. The trucks contain all the lights, stands, and equipment necessary to power the lights. "You want to get the trucks as close as logistically possible to the set," he says, "because there's an awful lot of hauling stuff around involved and the stuff can be pretty heavy."

Typically, the best boy works with the gaffer to devise the best way of going about setting up and powering the lighting equipment, and then delegates various jobs to various members of the lighting crew. The cable necessary to power the set with electricity is the first item of business, and crew members are assigned to run it to all the places that lighting or other electrical appliances will be necessary.

Once the cable is in place, the lights and equipment needed to secure them get unloaded, carried to where they need to be, and set up. All this must be done fairly quickly, because everyone is anxious to get the set ready and the filming underway.

"Once everything is in place it's a 10- or 12-hour shooting day," Haden says. "And then we haul everything back to the truck and load it back up."

He enjoys the job, but competition in the filming industry everywhere is tough, Haden says. The Dallas area has seen a decrease in location filming because many of the states surrounding Texas offer tax incentives for companies to film there.

"The work isn't as steady as it used to be," he says. "It can get a little tough sometimes. The tax breaks have made it more inviting for producers to go someplace else to film. It can be frustrating."

While Haden says his undergraduate degree is of value in his business, it's experience that he figures is the best teacher. Even someone who has a degree from a college or university should consider working in an internship position or be willing to jump into an entry level job to gain the much needed hands-on know-how. Because competition can make getting the job you want difficult, the more experience you have, the better, Haden advises.

Finally, he notes that it's important to learn that not getting a particular job doesn't mean you won't be successful down the road. The entertainment industry can be cutthroat, he says, and you'll do well not to take the inevitable bumps in the road personally. Just be willing to do whatever is required without complaining, and remember what you've learned. "A thick skin and good common sense are your best friends in this industry," Haden says. "Thick skin, common sense, and a great love of sleep deprivation."

boy to help make them happen how, and when, they're supposed to.

The job of best boy can vary tremendously, depending on who's producing the film and who's the head gaffer. Some gaffers use best boys as personal gophers, while others rely solely on the technical knowledge and willingness to help with equipment. Some gaffers depend on best boys to keep track of equipment and to help maintain it, while others prefer to do that sort of work themselves.

This means that one best boy job might be very, very different from another. Some films or videos are shot outdoors, while others will entail indoor work or a combination of both. Some filming is done at night; some, during the heat (or cold) of the day. Still others, such as commercials, are shot in a studio.

Pitfalls

As are many Hollywood jobs, many sets are unionized, so best boys must join so they can get more work (this is because some film productions use only union workers). However, depending on where you live and work, it can be difficult to find or to get into a film union. Competition for best boy jobs is fairly intense, so you may have to be patient and prepared to pound the pavement looking for work. You may have to take on some low paying jobs in order to break into the field and then work

your way up to better jobs. Because you're an underling to the gaffers, you need to be willing to take orders and do what you're told to do without complaining or arguing. Filming days are typically long days, easily ranging from 10 to 12 hours of hard work.

Perks

Being a best boy is a great way to learn the fine points of lights and lighting—it's like getting paid to go to school. While working in a job that you can use to move on to a higher position, you're still given substantial responsibility and authority. You also get to work with creative people in a variety of settings, and your workday is practically guaranteed to be interesting—every day.

Get a Jump on the Job

While you're still in high school, you can get involved with school theater productions and volunteer to do lighting. Move into community theater, where you may be able to work with a lights person who's had some training. If you have an arts school or institute in your town, check to see if they offer a theater or film light and sound course. Some internships are available in the area of production lighting, so check those out, too.

BOOM OPERATOR

OVERVIEW

The job of a boom operator is not just important—it's hard work. Boom operators manually or mechanically maneuver a microphone that's attached to a long pole, known as a *boom*, above the action of a scene. With either method, the boom operator must keep the microphone moving along with the action of a film or theater production in order to capture the conversation of the actors and actresses, as well as any music or audio sound effects. Boom operators also work on television news shows, documentaries, and reality shows.

Boom operators have to keep the microphone close enough to the action to record all the sound, but not so close that it can be seen on film. If the boom gets into the shot, the shot has to be redone. Operating the boom is especially challenging when one character is standing up while the other is sitting down, or there are crowd scenes with several or many people speaking at once. Operating a boom manually can be a physical strain, due to the weight of the microphone and length of time the operator must hold it.

If you're operating a mechanical boom, you sit on top of a platform that's about three feet high; from there, you operate a giant swivel, from which extends a telescoping steel arm that reaches about 40 feet into the air. At the end of the steel arm is a foot-long microphone, which you direct from your seat to record the action below.

AT A GLANCE

Salary Range

The median annual salary for the operator of a boom (a microphone attached to a long pole) is $36,970, with the lowest 10 percent earning less than $18,540 and the highest 10 percent earning more than $82,510. The average range is between $24,330 and $57,350 annually, according to government statistics.

Education/Experience

There are no specified educational requirements for a boom operator. Most, however, have completed at least a two-year program at a community college or have a degree in film, broadcasting, or theater from a college or university.

Personal Attributes

Must have good upper body strength (booms can be heavy) and a steady hand. You should have the ability to concentrate for extended periods of time, and, because it's often necessary to climb ladders in order to get microphones over scenes, you should be comfortable with heights.

Requirements

Knowledge of basic electronics and equipment used in audio work. Should have solid understanding of the fundamentals of sound and sound reproduction, and must have a basic understanding of various aspects of film or theater, such as wardrobe, how characters move, and how lines are delivered.

Outlook

The number of jobs for boom operators is expected to increase by between 10 and 20 percent through the year 2012, an average increase. Talented boom operators, however, may have less trouble finding work than those in other areas of the entertainment industry.

As a boom operator, you've got to know a fair amount about film or theater production, because you've got to be able to anticipate the actions and movement of the people on the set or stage. You also need to have an idea of the script so that you can keep up with who will be speaking and when. Operating a boom requires a tremendous amount of concentration and attention to what's happening on the stage or set. If you get distracted by something going on off the set, chances are good that the microphone won't be in place to record dialogue, or it will show up on film so that the shot has to be retaken.

Boom operators also are responsible for making sure the microphone doesn't cause shadows on the set. They're often required to help place additional microphones on the set and perform other set chores.

Along with all the work and stress, however, comes a fair amount of respect from other members of the production crew. Boom operators are important to the success of a show, film, or play, and most people are very well aware of that. There's always a place in a production for a good, experienced boom operator.

Pitfalls

As with many jobs in entertainment, it can be difficult to break into the field of boom

Nick Selby, former CBS boom operator

Nick Selby, 39, no longer works as a boom operator, but he clearly remembers the time that he did on the daytime series *As the World Turns* as being both fun and difficult. "A boom operator has an immensely challenging job that requires a sound knowledge of recording techniques, camera work, and lighting," he explains.

As boom operator on the set of a soap opera, he worked 10- to 12-hour days, usually starting at about 9 a.m. He operated a boom mechanically, which is not an easy thing to do.

"The task is to jab through space and stick the microphone towards the speaking actors on the set," Selby says, "getting close enough for good sound pickup, but keeping well out of the way of the camera shot. You need to swivel the live end of the directional microphone toward the actor speaking, all the while avoiding the labyrinth of overhead lights."

After attending the Institute for Audio Research in New York City for two years, Selby worked as a sound engineer in off-Broadway theatrical productions and in recording studios. Before moving to *As the World Turns*, he worked at CBS Sports as audio coordinator. His training as a boom operator came on the job from a veteran, which, he says, is a good way to learn the trade. Eventually, he moved on to the CBS-TV Broadcast Center studio.

While he enjoyed his work as a boom operator, there were some downsides to the job. "Imagine being forced to watch a television soap opera for 10 hours a day," he says. "And not just a soap—but one in which you must watch each scene two, three, or more times because the actors flub their lines, or cameras grab the wrong shots, or—and it happens—a boom gets in the shot."

Selby recommends that anyone interested in working as a boom operator find a school with a good audio program, and then break into the industry in whatever way possible in order to gain experience. An internship with a boom operator is a good way to learn the craft, but keen competition makes it almost necessary to get formal education, as well.

operation. Competition is keen for those just starting out. In addition, operating a boom often demands long, hard days of physically demanding work, and it can involve significant travel and time away from home.

Perks

Working as a boom operator can be immensely satisfying because you get to see the results of your hard work on a film or production. Boom operators also work close to the action and typically get to know performers, which many people find to be exciting.

Get a Jump on the Job

Volunteer in school or in your community to do any sort of job involving sound. You can work on your school's video crew, volunteer to do sound for class plays and musicals, volunteer at a local television station, or even make your own movies. Any type of work that provides experience with sound and sound equipment will benefit you down the road.

CAMERA OPERATOR

OVERVIEW

Where would the motion picture industry be if the director yelled "Action!" and nobody was there behind the camera to start filming? As important as the actor, producer, and director may be to a commercial, movie, or TV show, it's the camera operator whose skill is responsible for capturing the work of the other members of the creative team. Television, video, and motion picture camera operators produce images that tell a story, inform or entertain an audience, or record an event. There wouldn't be any movies, TV shows, or ads without them.

No matter how sophisticated video and camera equipment gets, making commercial-quality movies and video programs still requires quite a bit of technical expertise and creativity on the part of the camera operator. In order to produce successful images, you've got to select the appropriate equipment and apply a good eye and steady hand to assure smooth, natural movement of the camera. You've got to anticipate what's happening on the set or in the field, and be ready to capture the moment.

Camera operators use TV, video, or motion picture cameras to shoot a wide range of material, including television series, studio programs, news and sporting events, music videos, motion pictures, documentaries, and training sessions. Some camera operators film or videotape private ceremonies and special events. (Those who record images on videotape are often

AT A GLANCE

Salary Range

$14,710 to $65,070+. Median annual earnings for television, video, and motion picture camera operators are $32,720; the middle 50 percent earn between $20,610 and $51,000; the lowest 10 percent earned less than $14,710, and the highest 10 percent earned more than $65,070. Median annual earnings are $46,540 in the motion picture and video industries and $25,830 in radio and TV broadcasting. Wages are based on the camera operator's skill and reputation. Many camera operators who work in film or video are freelancers, so their annual earnings change from year to year. Benefits vary by employer; full-time camera operators receive vacation, sick leave, and health insurance. Many camera operators also are unionized, and receive better pay and benefits.

Education/Experience

Television, video, and motion picture camera operators usually have both on-the-job training and training at vocational schools, colleges, universities, or photographic institutes. Jobs with news teams at TV stations often require a bachelor's degree; most camera operators learn their skills at college, studying operation, photographic processes, and camera techniques. Many universities, community and junior colleges, vocational-technical institutes, and private trade and technical schools offer courses in camera operation and videography. Basic courses cover equipment, processes, and techniques.

Personal Attributes

Technical expertise, imagination, an eye for detail, patience, accuracy, attention to detail, and creativity are essential. Because camera operators typically must carry heavy equipment for hours on end, physical strength and endurance are required. If you're going to run your own businesses, you'll need business skills as well as talent, knowing how to submit bids, write contracts, get permission to shoot

(continues)

AT A GLANCE *(continued)*

on private locations, obtain releases to use film or tape of people, price your services, get copyrights, and keep financial records.

Requirements

Must have your own camera equipment, good eyesight, basic talent. Camera operators need good verbal skills in order to communicate with directors, actors, and technicians. They must also have the ability to hold a camera for long periods of time.

Outlook

Employment of camera operators is expected to grow about as fast as the average for all occupations through 2012. Rapid expansion of the entertainment market, especially motion picture production and distribution, will spur growth of camera operators. In addition, computer and Internet services will provide new outlets for interactive productions. Growth will be tempered, however, by the increased offshore production of motion pictures. Camera operators will be needed to film made-for-the-Internet broadcasts, such as live music videos, digital movies, sports features, and general information or entertainment programming. Job growth also is expected in radio and television broadcasting.

called videographers.) Many are hired by independent TV stations, local affiliates, large cable and television networks, or smaller, independent production companies. Studio camera operators work in a broadcast studio and usually videotape their subjects from a fixed position.

News camera operators (also called electronic news gathering [ENG] operators) typically work as part of a reporting team, following newsworthy events as they unfold. Capturing live events requires another whole set of skills, since you've got to anticipate the action in order to film it. ENG operators may need to edit raw footage on the spot for relay to a television affiliate for broadcast.

Camera operators who work in the entertainment field use motion picture cameras to film movies, TV programs, and commercials. (Those who film motion pictures are also known as cinematographers.) Some specialize in filming cartoons or handling special effects.

As a camera operator, you may be a part of the action, shooting whatever passes in front of the lens, or capturing the action from different angles with the camera mounted on a track. Other camera operators sit on cranes and follow the action while crane operators move them into position. Steadicam operators don a harness and carry the camera on their shoulders to provide a clear picture while they move about the action. More recently, digital cameras have enhanced the number of angles and the clarity that you can expect. Camera operators who work in the entertainment field often meet with directors, actors, editors, and camera assistants to discuss ways of filming, editing, and improving scenes.

About one out of every five camera operators work for themselves; some contract with TV networks, while others work as documentary or independent filmmakers, or for ad agencies, for trade show or convention sponsors. Most salaried camera operators work for TV stations or motion picture studios, more typically in urban areas.

In the film industry, it's usually who you know that can help you get a job, since you get hired based on recommendations from people the companies have worked with in the past. When you first start out, you'll probably work with more experienced camera operators; you'll learn how to set up lights, cameras, and other equipment. You may receive routine assignments requiring adjustments to their cameras or decisions on what subject matter to capture. Starting out in Hollywood can be tough, since many positions are union jobs. (Camera operators may belong to the International Alliance of Theatrical Stage Employees and the National Association of Broadcast Employees and Technicians.)

Once you get more experienced or join the union, you're usually hired for a project on the basis of recommendations from individuals such as producers, directors of photography, and camera assistants from previous projects, or through interviews with the producer. As you work closely with directors, technicians, and assistants, you may even be able to influence directors or performers in filming decisions. As you get more experience, you'll also be called on to supervise or train camera assistants.

ENG and studio camera operators who work for television affiliates usually

Simone Shoemaker, camera operator

Simone Shoemaker—an experienced camera operator and an independent producer, and owner of Coastline Productions—started out to study architecture in her native East Germany. However, a fascination with the world of photography took her in a completely new direction. Growing up in East Germany back before the country was unified, Simone Shoemaker was always magically attracted to anybody who carried a camera.

"I was studying architecture at the time when I just walked up to a guy who was shooting a news photo and I said: 'What are you doing? Can you show me how to do it?' He taught me darkroom work and how to use the camera." Shoemaker might have ended up as a news photographer, except that the next person she noticed lugging around a camera was using a video camera.

"I walked up to him and said: 'What are you doing? Can you show me how to do it?'" Shoemaker ended up marrying the videographer, who was an American on vacation in East Germany. He had an editing studio in his house, lived with the equipment, and taught Shoemaker the business.

"Filming was basically something I felt drawn to, in such a forceful way," she explains. "Architecture was no longer of interest."

Working in the United States for the past 15 years, Shoemaker spends her time as a freelance camera operator and producer for corporate clients. "Let's say they want to do a promotional video," she says. "I write the script, I figure out what I need to show, I edit, I do the whole shebang. That's the fun part."

The difficult part, she says, is landing a client in the first place. To keep working steadily, she also freelances as a camera operator for others who don't want to fly across the country to handle one interview. She also freelances for the audiovisual industry.

(continues)

start in small markets to gain experience. Gradually, you'll move on to more demanding assignments or to positions with larger or network TV stations. Advancement for ENG operators may mean you need to move to a larger media markets.

Some camera operators and editors may become directors of photography for movie studios, advertising agencies, or TV programs, whereas others teach at technical schools, film schools, or universities.

It may seem as if just about everybody you know wants a job on TV or in Hollywood, so it shouldn't be a surprise that there is keen competition for camera operator jobs. There are usually many more people who want a job than there are jobs to get. Those who manage to land a salaried job or get enough work to earn a living as a freelancer are typically the most creative, highly motivated, adaptable, and business-savvy people. Related work experience or job-related training also can help.

When you arrive on the set or on location, you'll determine the filming and lighting requirements, and then consult with the director about filming and lighting requirements and desired effects. Then you'll select the right cameras, accessories,

---

(continued)

"I don't do news," she says. "There are a couple of women camera operators, but they are very few. It's tough to carry a camera on your shoulder all day long, every day."

Being a freelancer is the tough part of the business, she says, "because you never know where your next job is coming from, and there is never enough work. I suppose it would be very different if I had a full-time job at a news station."

But still, she loves her work. "I get to stick my nose in different things every day," she explains. "It's just fascinating. One day I'll be on the roof of a high-rise shooting helicopters landing, and the next day I'm bathing a dog in the studio."

Shoemaker advises students to get used to the idea that they'll need to start out small, so they should get all the experience they need. "Nobody cares what you studied in school—you need to have the field experience," she says. "I've actually run into kids I hired as grips—as production assistants. They had this tremendous attitude—sort of 'I could be the next Steven Spielberg.' Well, with that attitude you're not going to get very far unless your granddaddy is Steven Spielberg."

To be a good camera operator, Shoemaker believes you have to have a natural feel for what a shot looks like, and how to frame the shot correctly. "I don't know if that can be learned," she says, "but it helps to run around and take photos and have somebody discuss it with you to see if you can develop something." When you move the camera, she notes, you should constantly check your framing to make sure what the camera sees always looks good. "That's very difficult for a lot of beginners, who see the beginning and ending shots, but they don't know how to get there along the way. If they are filming a speaker, they want to zoom out, but way too late they realize they have way too much sky. You need to keep in mind that it's basically 30 photos per second, and they all have to look good."

equipment, and film for filming, and set up cameras and equipment to produce the desired effects. (On large projects, you'll instruct camera assistants how to set up the equipment.) After filming, you may edit raw film footage on the scene for relay to a TV station for broadcast.

Pitfalls

Camera operators who work for government, TV and cable networks, and advertising agencies usually work a five-day, 40-hour week, but those filming movies may work much longer hours or travel to faraway locations for many months at a time. Some camera operators (especially those covering accidents, natural disasters, civil unrest, or military conflicts) may work in uncomfortable or dangerous surroundings. Many camera operators must wait long hours in all kinds of weather for an event to take place and must stand or walk for long periods while carrying heavy equipment. Because most freelance camera operators buy their own

equipment, it can cost a lot to buy and maintain cameras and accessories.

Perks

Handling a camera for a major motion picture or big-time TV show can be lots of fun—you're right there in the middle of the action. If you love to travel, don't have anything to tie you down, and you love the movie business, it can be an exciting career with lots of unpredictability and creativity.

Get a Jump on the Job

If you're interested in filming and handling cameras, try subscribing to videographic newsletters and magazines, join video or movie filming clubs, and try to get a part-time or summer job in cable and TV networks, motion picture studios, or camera and video stores. Look for internship programs while you are in school. These offer good experience and contacts.

CASTING DIRECTOR

OVERVIEW

One of the nice things about being a casting director is that there's always somebody who's hoping to meet you! A casting director serves as a liaison between aspiring actors, and the writers, producers, and directors of a play, commercial, or TV show. The casting director narrows the search for the producers and directors, who usually have the final say over who gets the part. Casting directors looking to hire actors for smaller roles and as extras usually hire on their own, without having to send the actor on for approval to producers and directors.

Casting directors must have many contacts who can recommend the best actors for particular parts. If a casting director doesn't have the right connections, the most desirable actors will work elsewhere. For that reason, if you want to be a casting director, it's extremely important to know how to network—because sometimes it's not what you know, but who you know. That certainly holds true in the entertainment industry.

Casting directors work with agents and managers, and are expected to build up their own files of actors and actresses who they can tap for parts that may be appropriate. New software makes it even easier to gain access to dozens of categories of actors, helping casting directors narrow their fields of possible characters.

Some casting directors are hired on a full-time basis by theaters or advertising agencies, and are responsible for finding

AT A GLANCE

Salary Range

The median salary is about $48,000 a year, with the middle 50 percent earning between $31,990 and $70,910. The highest 10 percent earn more than $120,000, and the lowest 10 percent earn less than $23,300, according to government figures.

Education/Experience

Casting directors come from various backgrounds and have different educational experience. Some train at theater schools as actors, while others study theater management or have business degrees. While some have landed jobs as casting directors without any formal education, an undergraduate degree in a related area is recommended.

Personal Attributes

Should be personable, and willing and able to initiate and maintain relationships with actors, agents, and other members of casting and production teams. Must have good networking skills and a keen sense for different qualities of actors and actresses that make them perfect for particular roles.

Requirements

A background in theater and some acting experience probably is necessary, as is an internship with a casting director. An internship is the only way to truly learn the job. Theater schools may have courses in casting, but they are very limited.

Outlook

The number of casting director jobs is expected to increase by between 10 and 20 percent through the year 2012. That job growth is considered to be average.

actors for TV commercials, print media, and live events. Sometimes, as when casting for a radio advertisement, a casting director may only be concerned with a person's voice. Many are freelance or contract employees who operate their own casting businesses and either move from one job to the next or work from their own offices. Freelance casting directors may work for production companies, directors, and production managers to seek out talented individuals for films, TV, voice-over work, and print media.

When it comes to selecting actors, a casting director has to be choosy. You can

Melisa Dugal, casting director

Melisa Dugal had always wanted to be an actor, but after her first child was born she left the stage and, by accident, became a casting director. While volunteering as director of special events at the Maine International Film Festival, a yearly event held in her hometown of Waterville, Maine, Dugal ran into a friend who had recently been hired to handle the locations casting for an HBO movie called *Empire Falls*. As luck would have it, her friend was looking for an assistant casting director.

"Lucky me!" Dugal says. "What followed was four months of the best training I could ever get. She taught me everything there is to know about being a casting director, and encouraged me to pursue casting as a career." Not long after that, Dugal started her own company, Access Actors, in Sidney, Maine—and she hasn't looked back.

The best things about being a casting director, she says, is being a part of the filmmaking process and having the opportunity to launch people into acting careers. "There is a very creative aspect of the job that appeals to me," she says. "When I'm not working on a specific project, I am always on the lookout for new faces. It's fun to try to match up specific talent to a certain part."

Dugal is a locations casting director, responsible for finding actors and actresses for smaller speaking roles, background extras, and stand-ins. She uses a variety of methods to round up talent, including open calls that are advertised through area newspapers and radio, online talent databases, and talent agencies.

Her responsibilities might include auditioning and pre-screening talent, handling union paperwork for the production, scheduling callbacks and call times, coordinating wardrobe fittings and so forth. It's important to be organized, Dugal says, especially when you're responsible for finding a lot of people. That results in an unbelievable number of details you've got to keep track of.

"My work is a process of finding the right people for a job, making sure they are properly prepared and getting them where they need to be when they need to be there," she explains. "That can be a daunting task if it's a film with several thousand extras!"

Still, Dugal says she's happy in casting, and intends to continue working in the field. Although she's busy, having her own company allows her some flexibility with family time, which is important to her. While she doesn't expect to join what she calls the "big time" casting directors whose names appear on the big screens, she's content with her work.

"As a casting director, people are always happy to hear from you," Dugal says. "You're the one getting them work and, in some cases, making dreams come true. That's a nice way to spend your day."

spend hours looking over files and Web sites, checking out photos and resumes of potential cast members. If you think an actor might be suitable for a particular part, you'll call the person in to read for the part. If it seems like a good fit, the actor will be asked to audition for the director, who normally has the ultimate say. Obviously, you must fully understand the character that you're casting, as well as the full scope of the show, play, or commercial. You'll typically spend a lot of time studying scripts in order to get as good a grasp on each character as possible. Because you want your choice of talent to impress the director and producers, you can bet that some pretty intense selection will occur.

Many casting directors move into the profession from acting, stage managing, or helping a producer or casting person. Because there's very little formal training available for casting directors, most have worked as a casting intern before moving into the job on their own. This may entail working for free, because there are many people looking for internships. Nearly all major casting directors belong to the national Casting Society of America (CSA), a professional association for casting directors located in Hollywood.

Pitfalls

There aren't a lot of casting director jobs, so there's lots of competition. In fact, the job is so competitive that people are willing to intern for free for months in order to learn the business. And because there's constant pressure for casting directors to always know the right people and have the proper connections, some people in the field burn out.

Perks

Just think, you might be the casting director who discovers the next Johnny Depp or Hilary Swank! Casting is an important job in the entertainment industry, and it can be exciting. If you like networking and meeting new people, you'll probably enjoy a job as a casting director. Because movies, documentaries, commercials, and other productions are filmed all over the world, there's work for casting directors in locations far beyond New York City or the West Coast.

Get a Jump on the Job

Because networking skills are so important to a casting director, you should start working on those skills now. Check out books on how to network and make contacts. Then practice your newfound skills by making new contacts in your school or community. Some knowledge of acting and production is also important, so it's a good idea to get involved with school or community theater, or a local TV station.

CELEBRITY ASSISTANT

OVERVIEW

There are as many types of celebrity assistants as there are celebrities, and their roles vary tremendously. Celebrity assistants might work for actors or actresses, rock stars, motivational speakers, best-selling authors, politicians, professional athletes, directors, top-notch lawyers, or wealthy families. They might work round-the-clock or part time, and live on premises or off. They may travel constantly with the celebrity, or rarely travel at all. And the day-to-day duties they're expected to perform vary tremendously.

If you're looking at becoming a celebrity assistant, you first should target the type of celebrity you would like to assist. Attempt to match your skills and expertise to a celebrity with whom you'd be compatible and could be especially helpful. If you're a professional party planner who's looking to become a celebrity assistant, for instance, it would make more sense for you to work for someone who's very social and loves to give parties than for someone who tends to be reclusive. In other words, it pays to do your homework before seeking or accepting a position as a celebrity assistant. Most people who want to be celebrity assistants are lured to the job because of a desire to live and work close to a celebrity.

A personal assistant is expected to perform tasks that make the life of his or her employer easier. Some personal assistants cook, take clothes to the dry cleaner, shop for groceries, take care of kids, and walk

AT A GLANCE

Salary Range

$30,000 to more than $100,000 a year, depending on the celebrity, location, job requirements, benefits, perks, and other factors.

Education/Experience

There are no educational requirements to be a celebrity assistant, although some celebrities might insist on a college degree. Others may want someone with a background in business, public relations, marketing, or other related area.

Personal Attributes

It is imperative that you are discreet and able to maintain confidentiality. You also must be resourceful, able to withstand criticism, patient, organized, and adept at networking.

Requirements

You probably will be required to have a valid driver's license. You must be able to write effectively and should have good computer skills. Most celebrities want their assistants to be nice looking (although not nicer looking than themselves), well groomed, and well dressed. You must be poised and able to present yourself well in various situations, including business and social events.

Outlook

There are more and more celebrities all the time, so the need for celebrity assistants is expected to increase. Also, there tends to be a high turnover of celebrity assistants, making entry into the field easier to attain.

the dog for their celebrities. Others are primarily responsible for answering mail, scheduling appointments, and screening phone calls. The realm of responsibilities the job may entail is tremendous.

Some celebrity assistants remain in the business for the long haul, while others use the position as a means to an end. If someone wants to be a film director, for instance, he or she might try to land a job as a personal assistant to a director in order to gain access to the director's knowledge and business contacts. While there's nothing wrong with that technique—you could look at it as a sort of internship experience—you probably should be up front with your employer concerning your aspirations.

Celebrity assistants are generally a resourceful lot, and for good reason. If your employer insists on a special dry cleaning technique that's only available in two shops in the entire city, you'd better know how to find out which shops offer the service. Celebrity assistants tell stories

Mary Langford, celebrity assistant

Mary Langford has always dreamed of being a famous actress. While she hasn't given up that dream, she's biding her time for the moment as a celebrity assistant in Los Angeles and Palm Springs.

While Langford isn't able to name her employer, she did reveal that he's "an extremely high-profile writer" who has written for Broadway and film, and also has a few novels to his credit.

Langford came to be a celebrity personal assistant in a rather roundabout way, like many celebrity assistants. "We all get to where we are by different paths," she says. "My path was that of being a court reporter."

A court reporter is the person who uses a machine during a trial to record all the conversation. Langford was a court reporter for 16 years before she moved to Hollywood, vowing that she'd never again perform the job unless it was on a TV show or in a movie. Sure enough, she was cast as a court reporter in several shows and movies, including the television series *Murder One*, which ran from 1995 until 1997, and the 2001 movie *I Am Sam*, which starred Sean Penn and Michelle Pfeiffer. "That was great, but really, I was doing the same thing I'd been doing before I moved to Hollywood," Langford says. "I decided to look for other kinds of roles."

One morning, when Langford was looking at classified ads in a Hollywood trade magazine, she came across an ad listed by a best-selling author who was looking for a court reporter to serve as his personal assistant. The idea was for him to dictate his writing to the assistant, who would record and transcribe the work. Langford decided to apply for the job.

"We hit it off immediately and I've been working for him for four years now," Langford says.

Langford's employer has homes in both Los Angeles and Palm Springs, so she divides her time between those cities. When she's in LA, she lives with her husband in their home, but when she's in Palm Springs, she stays in quarters on the author's property. She has an agreement with her employer for time off when she gets called to an acting audition.

"Whenever the phone rings for an audition, I get to go," she says. "But that's very unusual. Most assistants are expected to be available 24/7. Most celebrities are pretty demanding and when they want something, they want it now."

of employers calling at 3 a.m. to request that the assistant locate and deliver a particular type of ice cream—"And make it snappy!" Being able to find out that the all-night convenience store down the street stocks Ben & Jerry's New York Super Fudge Crunch might just save your job—or at least allow you to deliver the ice cream and get back to bed!

Working for a famous person has its ups and downs, according to those who perform the job. While some celebs are laid-back and down to earth, others tend to be a little eccentric. For that reason, many celebrity assistants go into the job thinking it's going to be the best experience they've ever had, only to discover they're in over their heads.

While Langford's primary responsibility is recording and transcribing her employer's writing, she also handles scheduling, screens and answers phone calls, helps plan trips for the author and his wife, handles correspondence, and so forth. Normally, she works five days a week, but if her employer is in the middle of a book or other writing project, all bets are off.

"There was a four-month stretch where I worked 10 to 12 hours a day for 22 days straight," Langford says. "But my employer compensated me well." Her celebrity, who Langford calls "one in a trillion," on several occasions has given her generous bonuses, including an envelope that contained fifty $100 bills.

It's very important, she says, to know your employer's preferences and priorities so you can best serve him or her. "You are the person who protects the celebrity from the outside world," Langford says. "So, I need to know when my employer is eating lunch and there's a call from so-and-so, if he would want to have his lunch interrupted to take the call. In some cases, he definitely would want to be interrupted. But in other cases, I'll take a message and tell him about the call once he's finished eating."

It's also important to have good communication skills and be organized, she says. If you find it difficult to keep a myriad of details in your head, including names, dates, and numbers, you should take detailed notes of what occurs and when. One of the most important qualifications of a good celebrity assistant is being able to keep your mouth shut.

"Discretion is extremely important," Langford says. "The vast majority of celebrity assistants sign confidentiality agreements and are very restricted in what they can say and can't say. But even if you don't have an agreement, it's not a good idea to be saying things you shouldn't."

Langston advises anyone who gets a job as a celebrity assistant to join a networking organization such as the Los Angeles-based Association of Celebrity Personal Assistants, for which she is a spokesperson. Belonging to such an organization provides valuable tools to help on the job, she says.

Langston, who is still waiting to be vaulted to stardom in her acting career, says she doesn't know how long she'll remain in her current position. But, she says, it's been thoroughly enjoyable, and a great learning experience. "I've been really fortunate to be able to be involved in every part of his writing process," she says. "I don't know where all this will take me, but we'll see. I think I've been very, very lucky."

Even those celebrity assistants who run screaming from their jobs after a couple of years, however, admit that there are some great advantages. Many personal assistants travel with their employers, enjoying private planes, five-star hotels, and fine meals along the way. Some are given generous clothing allowances, because it's important to their employers that the assistants look great. Some celebrities have more than one assistant, creating the opportunity for camaraderie to develop.

While working as a celebrity assistant isn't for everyone, it does have the potential to be an exciting, once-in-a-lifetime experience. Because celebrities tend to have lots of contact with other celebrities, you never know who you might meet or where the job might take you.

Pitfalls

Long hours, demanding employers, and the necessity of being at your employer's beck and call all the time can make the job of celebrity assistant sound downright unappealing. There will be days when you feel that your life is not your own. Unfortunately, that's part of the territory.

Perks

Many celebrities really appreciate when their assistants go the extra mile for them, and are willing to reward them handsomely for doing so. You're likely to get to meet celebrities other than your employer, and often, there's travel included with the position. If you live on your employer's property, your accommodations are likely to be pretty cushy, and you'll be gaining life experience—and with luck, a Rolodex full of contacts.

Get a Jump on the Job

Work to develop skills such as recording daily events, remembering names and being able to match them to faces, being organized and efficient, and being able to comfortably talk to all kinds of people. Start researching the lifestyles of different celebrities so you might get an idea of how they live. There also are books and some seminars available on becoming a celebrity assistant. Check the appendixes of this book for more information.

CELEBRITY PHOTOGRAPHER

OVERVIEW

As long as there are celebrities, there'll be a need for celebrity photographers. These are the photographers who take publicity shots for actors and actresses, models, and other famous people. Some specialize in glamour shots, while others photograph top-level executives for photos that will be issued to news magazines and used in annual reports and other company literature. Celebrity photographers might photograph musicians, motivational speakers, politicians, TV personalities, rock stars, movie stars, famous authors, or sports celebrities. Celebrity photographers offer their services to *ordinary* clients as well.

But there's much more involved with being a celebrity photographer than just pointing a camera and clicking the shutter button. Most celebrity photographers work out of studios, although some prefer to take photos in the celebrity's home or workplace, or another site that the photographer feels is appropriate (often, the location will depend on the type of photos to be taken.) It would be difficult, for instance, to set up in a photography studio for the famous *Sports Illustrated* swimsuit model shots—the very nature of the photographs requires that they be taken in natural, outdoor settings. Photographs for celebrities interviewed in *People* magazine, for example, are almost always taken at the celebrity's home. However, many photographers prefer studio work because they have better control over lighting, backgrounds, and so forth.

AT A GLANCE

Salary Range

While government figures show the average rate for all photographers to be about $29,000 a year, a well-known and sought-after celebrity photographer can make much, much more. One New York City-based photographer who offers digital photography head shot sessions for actors and actresses charges $600 plus tax per session, which results in 150 to 200 digital photos. A Chicago-based head shot photographers offers a one-hour studio session and one 8x10 portrait for $200.

Education/Experience

While there are no formal educational requirements for celebrity photographers, most have studied photography and many have degrees in photography, fine arts, or a related topic. If you'll be handling the business end of a celebrity photography service, it will be to your benefit to have had some education in the business area, as well.

Personal Attributes

Not only must photographers be artistically talented, they must also be able to work effectively with clients. It helps to be fairly outgoing and personable, since you'll need to promote your services. You need to be able to communicate effectively with clients so you can understand their expectations and convey your ideas. You also must be able to make people on the other side of the camera feel comfortable and at ease. Let's face it. Even celebrities get a little nervous when they're having their pictures taken!

Requirements

You'll need studio space and your own equipment, unless you decide to rent equipment.

Outlook

Photographer jobs are expected to increase by between 10 and 20 percent through the year 2012. That job growth is considered to be average, according to government figures.

Some celebrity photographers specialize in head shots, photographs of a client's head and shoulders, sort of like high school yearbook photos. Other photographers specialize in full-body shots. Some might work exclusively with black-and-white film. More and more celebrity photographers are turning to digital photography, which eliminates the need for using and processing more expensive camera film.

Typically the celebrity photographer and client confer—either in person or over the phone—a week or two before the photography session is to take place. During that meeting, the photographer and celebrity will discuss the purpose of the photo shoot. The photographer probably will ask what the pictures will be used for, to whom they'll be distributed, and the goal of the shot. The photographer may suggest the sort of clothing the celebrity should wear, perhaps recommending colors and fabrics that photograph well.

Most photographers have a menu of fees and services, charging certain amounts for different services. They'll charge more, for instance, if the client wants to be photographed in six different outfits

John Hart, celebrity head shot photographer

If you can name a celebrity who's been famous for the past 20 years, John Hart has probably snapped that picture. His client list includes Al Pacino, Dudley Moore, Jason Alexander, Kevin Bacon, Debra Monk, Bronson Pinchot, Roberta Peters, Christopher Lloyd, Robert Townsend, Jeff Daniels, Andrea McCardle, Bobby Collins, Christine Lahti, and Hal Holbrook.

The secret to his success, Hart says, is that he loves to work with people, and he can connect with his clients to understand what's unique and personal about them. "I'm able to reach inside their psyches and find something special that they have to communicate to others, and then make that appear in the photography."

Hart, who specializes in head shots and normally works with black and white film, also is noted for his lighting techniques. The author of several books on photography and lighting techniques, Hart works extensively with light. The results are apparent in his work. "An effective head shot should have three dimensions to it, like you see in major films and the well-lit soaps," Hart says. "It should never read flat and boring."

While many photographers are moving toward digital cameras, Hart continues to use a traditional version. He does not, however, develop his own film. "I've always used a professional lab to do my darkroom work," he says. "I have claustrophobia, so a darkroom isn't a good place for me. And I really don't have time, anyway. I factor the cost of the developing into my fee."

When working with a client, Hart does everything he can to make sure the person is relaxed and at ease. First he schedules a preliminary meeting to discuss issues such as wardrobe, hair, and makeup. During that time, he closely observes the client to pick up the most interesting aspects of the celebrity's personality, best features, and so forth. When it's time for the actual photo shoot, Hart makes sure that he's upbeat and positive.

rather than in just one set of clothing. The price of the photo shoot normally includes processing fees, and usually a certain number of prints of a specified size. Additional prints will cost more, and the photographer may also charge additional fees for touch-up work, enlargements, and other services. Celebrity photographers often work with particular wardrobe and makeup experts, although their clients may ask to use someone else for those services.

Anyone can hang out a shingle and declare him or herself a celebrity photographer. Until you've had some experience and people in the business begin to know who you are, you'll probably find yourself with very few customers. As a result, celebrity photographers pay to be listed on directories, and they may do extensive advertising until they are "discovered."

Pitfalls

While many photographers bill themselves as celebrity photographers and a fair number make a decent living from the job, the field is competitive and only a few

"I greet the client at the door in a friendly, receptive mood," Hart says. "It's very important to keep the client relaxed and relating to the camera as though it were a friend of theirs."

With four wardrobe changes, a photo shoot takes several hours and can become tiring. Hart takes about 18 shots for each change of wardrobe, working with the client to evoke various looks and emotions. It's important, he says, to get the client smiling on some images, and semi-serious on others.

While it's important for a head shot photographer to have a sense of humor and be able to make the client smile and feel comfortable, the photographer must not be tempted to make him or herself prominent, Hart says. "Remember that the client is the star, not the photographer," he advises.

While Hart always enjoyed photography, he started his career as an elementary and high school teacher. He earned a master's degree from Notre Dame University and now, in addition to running his head shot photography business, teaches a photography course at New York University and an "art of the storyboard" course at Columbia University. Being able to schedule clients as he wishes makes it possible for him to teach and pursue other endeavors that he enjoys, Hart says.

If you are interested in becoming a celebrity photographer, he suggests you read everything about photography and photographers. Look for a reputable school that offers a photography course, and see if you can become an assistant to a professional photographer. Then observe the characteristics and features of others, and try to figure out how you might best catch them on film.

Once you've become a celebrity photographer, there is one more thing to remember, Hart says. "It's your job to make people look good," he says. "That's what I really love!"

people make it really big. It can be tough to get started as an independent celebrity photographer because you need to have equipment and a place to work, which can cost a lot of money. And in order to be a successful celebrity photographer, you have to set up shop in an area where there are celebrities. If you were off the beaten path, you'd have to be *really* good for a big-time celebrity to travel to your studio.

Perks

Most photographers enjoy taking pictures, which means they get to make money by doing something they like. Even better, celebrity photographers get to meet and spend time with celebrities. If you've got a yen to meet famous people, and you've got a talent for the camera, then this could be the job for you.

Get a Jump on the Job

Take photography classes at your school or at a community college or arts school in your area. Read books written by people who are established celebrity photographers. Practice taking pictures of people. Set up a "studio" in your house and ask your friends and family to be your subjects. Some professional photographers offer private or group lessons. That information normally is included on their Web sites.

CLOWN

OVERVIEW

A big nose, wild hair, floppy shoes, and a horn—what's not to love? Most people associate clowns with circuses, but there actually are a variety of clowns who have traditionally performed under different circumstances. And lest you think of clowning as a modern art form, it actually has been going on for thousands and thousands of years.

A pygmy clown was thought to have performed as a jester in a pharaoh's court in Egypt in about 2500 B.C., while court jesters performed in China nearly 2,000 years before the birth of Christ. When Cortes conquered the Aztecs, there were clowns in Montezuma's court; so entrancing did Cortes find these entertainers that he carried some of the odd assortment of dwarfs and hunchbacks back to Spain with him. Most Native American tribes also had some form of clown character among them, some of whom were thought to have healing powers.

Traditionally, there are four popular types of clown: Whiteface, Hobo (or another type of character clown), Auguste, and New Vaudeville. Whiteface clowns, as the name implies, cover their faces with white makeup. One type of Whiteface (referred to as "neat") uses minimal face makeup and wears white clothing. The other type ("grotesque") wears very exaggerated clothing and may enlarge features such as ears or hair.

Hobo clowns—also known as tramp clowns—dress in tattered clothing, usually carrying hobo packs twisted around sticks

AT A GLANCE

Salary Range

How much money a professional clown can make depends on where he or she works, the type of clowning, and other factors. Circus clowns generally only earn between $200 and $300 a week, but receive housing, insurance, and other benefits. A freelance clown who performs at birthday parties and other events may be able to charge $200 an hour or more, depending on ability, reputation, location, and experience.

Education/Experience

There are no formal educational requirements for clowns, and people come into clowning from all walks of life. People who work as clowns vary from high school dropouts to people with advanced degrees and professional experience of nearly every kind. There are arts schools, circus schools, and clown schools where aspiring clowns can learn technique, study costuming, and so forth.

Personal Attributes

A professional clown must have excellent body and facial control. You must be able to connect with and to read your audience, knowing when something you're doing is working and when it isn't. You should have an outgoing personality and be able to get along well with others.

Requirements

You'll need to have props and equipment. In some municipalities, you might need a permit if you plan to perform in public places. You'll also need reliable transportation to travel to jobs and a valid driver's license or someone to transport you.

Outlook

Jobs in the field of clowning are expected to increase by between 10 and 20 percent through the year 2012. That job growth is considered to be average, according to government statistics.

as handles. Hobo clowns fall under the category of character clowns, which also can include firefighters, cowboys, and policemen. The job of a character clown—the most realistic looking of the three main clown forms—is to bring humor to the human condition and allow people to laugh at themselves and others.

Auguste clowns wear mismatched, oversized clothing; brightly colored wigs;

Daniel G. Chan, professional clown

Daniel Chan is a serious clown. He's also a magician, juggler, and acrobat who can breathe fire, and he's performed at trade shows, hospitality suites, restaurants, weddings, colleges, universities, and company parties. He also clowns at birthday parties, libraries, community events, and schools.

A graduate of the San Francisco School of Circus Arts, Chan is proud of the work he does and eager to set the record straight about clowns and clowning. "Clowning is a complicated art form," he explains. "A lot of people think that acting stupid is clowning, but it's not. Clowning is an art form with direction."

People who hang out a shingle offering clowning services without getting any training give the clowning profession a black eye, Chan says. "Plenty of people go into clowning without training, and that's not a good thing," he says. "You have to know what you're doing. Clowning isn't just about making people laugh, although that's important. You want to be able to touch the human spirit with clowning."

The secret of a funny clown, Chan says, is that he or she makes a mistake, and then repeats it over and over, using exaggerated motions and body language. Audiences identify with and respond to human frailty, Chan says, and can see themselves in the antics and actions of the clown. "Clowns are in all of us," he says. "That's what makes them funny."

Chan's first clowning jobs were making balloon sculptures for kids at parties and community events. Eventually, he added magic tricks, juggling, and acrobatics. As he became more well known, people started calling him, and he started offering his services to corporations, as well as schools, private parties, and community groups. Within a three-month period in 2005, Chan was booked for 37 events at libraries, art museums, learning centers, and churches. That doesn't mean there weren't some slow periods when he spends his days working on his acts, waiting for the phone to ring. "Some weeks you'll do nothing," he warns. "I've heard that good entertainers can do 500 shows a year. I'm not there yet, but I'm going to keep working."

Chan also will keep working on the business end of his business, which includes record keeping, taxes, billing, and marketing. As he becomes more well known, he's tapped for interviews and he tries not to turn any of them down. He stays in touch with instructors, mentors, and peers in the entertainment business, maintaining contact and relationships as he seeks to build new ones.

If it sounds like something you'd like to do, you need to spend some time learning the craft. "You have to learn about the clown tradition and clown culture," Chan says. "You can't just decide to become a clown, because that's what makes people not take the art of clowning seriously. Learn everything you can and never stop working to develop your skills."

big noses that might honk; and often have shoes that extend far past their feet. Ronald McDonald is an example of an Auguste clown.

The New Vaudeville clown wears no makeup, but entertains the audience by using a mixture of skills, including magic tricks, juggling, acrobatics, and mime. New Vaudeville clowns are typically found in specialized acts such as Cirque du Soleil.

If you're considering clowning as a career, what you'll need to know is that clowning is much more than simply getting in front of an audience and acting foolish or silly. Clowning involves planned, detailed actions that are designed to make people laugh and to involve the audience in the act. Most clowns have attended professional clown schools to learn the art of clowning before putting on their crazy costumes and getting out there in front of a crowd.

Circus clowning offers lots of jobs for professional clowns who are willing to travel. Ringling Brothers Circus divides its personnel into two groups, who alternate performances in the western and eastern portions of the United States. While the pay is generally low, the job is attractive because you get to travel and see the country, and you do receive benefits, such as health insurance. Clowns employed by organization such as Cirque du Soleil earn more than circus clowns, but must go through extensive auditioning processes. Those who get the job work very hard and undergo rigorous training.

Birthday party clowns perform at parties and other social events, or entertain before school audiences, civic groups, and community groups. Some clowns perform for free at carnivals, Renaissance fairs, or street fairs, depending on tips for their pay.

Many professional clowns who work birthday parties and other events also hold down full-time jobs on the side, because most find it hard to make enough money to support themselves. Sometimes, a birthday party clown will also offer party planning services, which means the clown plans and supplies everything needed for the party, including clowning services. Other clowns become well enough established so that they're busy all the time and don't need to work elsewhere.

If you want to be a professional clown, you need to remember that there's a business side to clowning, as well, and you'll need to know how to attend to matters such as billing and taxes. It's also very important that you know how to market yourself. You can be the best clown in the world, but if no one knows you're around, what does it matter? You'll need to keep lists of clients and potential clients with contact information, dates of performances, and rates.

Clowning can be a fun and rewarding career, but you'll need to be willing to put in a lot of work to prepare, practice, and perfect an act, and then add and revise it as your skills improve or your audiences change. Clowning is an ongoing process of learning and honing skills and developing new routines and acts.

Pitfalls

Clowns require costumes, a fair number of props, and other equipment, which can add up to a sizeable investment to get started. Regular work can be uncertain, at least until you've gotten established and built up a reputation. Family and friends could be unhappy about your dream because it's not considered a traditional career. You should remember, however, that clowning is a form of art. Once people realize the complexities of clowning, they tend to have more respect for the profession.

Perks

If you love to travel and meet lots of interesting people, the job of a circus clown could be right up your alley. Clowns get to have fun while they work, which is more than many people can say about their jobs. Having your own clowning business will allow you to have some flexibility with your schedule and get to be your own boss. Most people who work as clowns do so at least partially because they enjoy being around people and making them laugh.

They are entertainers who take their jobs seriously and like the results they see.

Get a Jump on the Job

If you're serious about learning to be a clown, check out clown schools, conferences, and workshops. Some communities have clown clubs that help potential clowns learn the business. There also are some good books that can teach you about makeup, face painting, magic tricks, balloon art, and other clown-related topics. Once you've learned some of the tricks of the trade, you might look for a professional clown who would let you work as an intern. Spending significant time with someone in the profession would give you a chance to see firsthand what a clown does, and help you to learn the skills necessary for clowning.

COMEDIAN

OVERVIEW

Jay Leno has his monologue. David Letterman has his "Top 10" list. Jim Carrey has his rubber face. Steve Martin has the arrow through his skull. Whoopi Goldberg has her wry observations. Each one of these comedians is funny in a unique, instantly recognizable way, and while it may look effortless, it's the product of years of practice, loads of talent, a keen mind, a bright wit, and a little luck.

Every known culture has its own form of comedy, and the ability to smile and laugh is hardwired into the human brain. If you've got a knack for jokes, or a dead-dry wit, you probably get a thrill out of making people laugh. Lots of others just like you have taken that raw talent and developed a unique style, skill, and body of work as an entertainer, either as a solo comedian or in a comedy troupe.

If you're in a comedy troupe, you develop, perform, and publicize your own material while working a day job to put food on the table. The troupe typically hosts a weekly show, with extra time spent rehearsing and critiquing each other's sketches and performances. Because you've got to listen to your peers' criticism, you'll need to be able to work well with others if you're going to succeed in a troupe. Troupes are typically found in urban areas where comedians congregate.

Solo comedians perform in clubs around the country, usually appearing one comedian after another each night. Solo stand-up comics face a significant level of unpleasant competition with other solos

AT A GLANCE

Salary Range

Varies a great deal depending on type of job, ranging from nothing (new comedians work in clubs for free) to midline acts earning between $50 and $75 for a half hour, with top acts earning $125 to $200 for 30 minutes to more than $1,000 per show; the most famous nationally known comedians may earn more than $25,000 a show.

Education/Experience

No specific education is required; some successful comedians have studied political science, journalism, acting, or comedy writing in workshops, seminars, or college coursework.

Personal Attributes

Ability to write, articulate, outgoing, determined, ability to work hard and persevere, ability to handle rejection, quick-witted, able to think on your feet, dedicated, and lucky.

Requirements

Good sense of humor, ability to communicate and connect with an audience.

Outlook

Fair. Fewer stand-up comedians are working and all are working for less money.

while they all study each other's material, style, pace, delivery, and presence.

Most comics start out playing for free in very small clubs or dingy nightclubs, or opening for bigger comedy acts or music acts.

As many as 30 percent of comedians slide into acting, where they face much the same odds against success. Others channel their creativity into advertising, teaching, or writing. The skills associated with comedy—the ability to make others laugh,

Charlie Hall, stand-up comedian

Charlie Hall didn't start out being a funny guy. In fact, it was his best friend who regularly cracked their classmates up—and after years of listening to the jokes, some of it started to rub off when he went away to college at the Rhode Island School of Design. "I think I got my sense of humor through osmosis," Hall explains. "My best friend was just so funny! When I got to college, I'd picked up his sense of humor. I used to make the kids in painting class laugh." By Hall's junior year in college, he was a hit at the school's faculty roast; from there, Hall moved on to a comedy night at a club in Newport, Rhode Island, and from there he moved on to a club in Boston.

Although a natural artist, after college he realized he really wanted to concentrate on making people laugh. In the early '80s, he talked the owner of a restaurant into trying a comedy night, which then became so popular that the restaurateur began holding comedy nights almost every evening. "Then some Boston guy saw me, and said I should show myself to more people, so I started working all around New England. I went from being an opening act to a midline act to a headline act."

In 1992, he was one of three comedians from Boston chosen to appear on the *MTV Half Hour Comedy Hour*, which lead to other shows. "The next year I got *Evening at the Improv* and then I made the semi-finals of *Star Search*. And then I got to work with my idol, Jerry Seinfeld. I was his middle act one week in New Haven, I got to hang out with him all weekend." Since then, Hall has also performed on *The Joan Rivers Show*, *Caroline's Comedy Hour*, *America's Funniest People*, and *Star Search '93*, where he was named a semi-finalist, and has performed as the opening act for comedian Sam Kinison and singers and musicians including Frankie Valli, Reba McIntire, Charlie Daniels, Chicago, Natalie Cole, B.B. King, and The Temptations.

But stand-up is only one of his many humor hats. He's also the creative force behind the long-running Rhode Island musical comedy cabaret *Ocean State Follies*, voted best comedy show by *Rhode Island Monthly Magazine* three times, and he's producing the second annual

to defuse tense situations with a well-timed remark, and to think on one's feet—are invaluable assets in any other career.

Pitfalls

A comedian works long hours for little (if any) pay, and endures enormous uncertainty, never knowing where the next paycheck will be coming from. The average beginning stand-up comedian earns about $50 for two 20-minute sets at a comedy club. While this translates into a solid hourly wage, a new comedian may perform only four sets a week, spending the rest of the time writing material, watching other comedians, and juggling other jobs to put food on the table. Failure, disappointment, and rejection are quite common; so common, in fact, that more than half of all new comedians don't last two years. In addition, the schedule can be rough for a stand-up comedian; it's not unusual for an aspiring stand-up comic to log more than 200 days per year away from home.

Perks

If you're a comedian, you were probably born with the ability to crack other people

Rhode Island Comedy Festival. He's written a similar show for Massachusetts audiences (*Mass Hysteria*). In his spare time, he's returned to his artistic origins and creates two political cartoons a week that appear in a number of Rhode Island newspapers, featuring local issues. In exchange, he gets free ads for his comedy shows. "I was originally going to be an illustrator and painter," he says, "but I've married the two talents, and now I also do political cartoons—I'm putting two talents to work for me."

His advice to potential comics is to be persistent—both in trying to find a place to perform and in writing the comedy bits. "Don't give up," he says. "If something isn't funny, you have to be persistent. Try to find your own place to appear. If nobody else has a comedy night, go to a restaurant and ask them to start one. Do comedy for free at first if you have to."

The toughest part about being a beginner stand-up comic is that sometimes you have to open for a famous act—and the audience isn't there to hear your comedy. "It's tough to open for a music act," he says, "because the people there aren't interested in seeing comedy. That's when you think: Why do I bother doing this?"

That's what happened the night he opened for blues guitarist B.B. King. "People were throwing drinks at me," he sighs. "You've signed a contract to do 45 minutes, and you have to stay on stage." A comedian thinks of the work as a craft, spending hours on preparation, so if the crowd is drunk or preoccupied during a performance, it's frustrating. But just when you start to wonder if you've picked the wrong profession, you'll have a good night when your jokes are hot and the crowd is appreciative.

"Let's say you perform at an official comedy club, with people who are there to see comedy. Everything works, and you come off the stage and you think, 'I get paid for that?' It's unbelievable!"

up—and the ability to stand up in front of a crowd and make strangers laugh can be an incredibly powerful, invigorating feeling.

Get a Jump on the Job

You'd be surprised by how many comedians say they got their start by being the class clown. If this sounds like you, or you just love to entertain and to make people laugh, you should get as much experience in front of an audience as you can while you're still in school. Volunteer to emcee your school shows. Participate in talent shows. If there are local comedy clubs or nightclubs where you live, find out when their "open mike" nights are scheduled, when comedians can try out new material. Practice your act at home and work on your material. Take any summer courses at local colleges or theaters in stand-up comedy or improvisation. Watch other comedians perform live as often as you can, and study their timing, topics, and delivery. Videotape your act so you can judge how you come across.

DIRECTOR OF PHOTOGRAPHY

OVERVIEW

Who's that person standing right behind the director, making sure the film looks great and making creative decisions left and right? It's the director of photography, probably one of the most important people on a film set. Even before shooting begins—a period of time that's called *preproduction*—the director will hunker down with the director of photography to discuss everything the camera is going to see—the look of the movie, shots, framing, lighting, even the emotion and the atmosphere that the director is going for.

Once everybody gets to the set, it's the director of photography's job to make sure the crew comes up with exactly what the director wants. It's up to the director of photography to decide on the scene lighting, shots, angles, lenses, tracks, and where the cameras are going to be positioned.

Directors of photography should be good at math, because part of the job involves reading charts and computing ratios to determine required lighting, film, shutter angles, filter factors, camera distance, depth of field and focus, and angles of view to produce the desired effects.

Directors of photography also need to work closely with the chief electrician to establish lighting requirements. They need to select the right cameras, accessories, equipment, and film stock, using their knowledge of filming techniques and requirements.

AT A GLANCE

Salary Range

Median annual earnings of salaried director of photography range from less than $23,300, to more than $119,760.

Education/Experience

Degree from film school or college majoring in film.

Personal Attributes

Patience, ability to work closely with others.

Requirements

Talent in visualization and in photography, artistic sense.

Outlook

Fair; the ranks of photography directors are fairly small, and the position is extremely competitive and likely to remain so.

Once all that has been done, directors of photography instruct the camera operators as to which camera setups, angles, distances, and movement they're looking for, and signal cues for starting and stopping filming. They also need to keep an eye out on set for potential problems, observing the effects of lighting, measuring lighting levels, and coordinating necessary changes.

Once the day's been filmed, they watch the film after processing and make adjustments as necessary to get the effects they want.

Of course, you don't graduate from high school and expect to land a gig as a director of photography (DOP). Get a degree in media studies or a related subject, or head for film school. Working on films is incredibly competitive, and most production companies won't take you seriously unless you have film to show them and qualifications—and a degree will get you both.

Once you graduate, you'll need to get a job as a "runner" or a clapper-loader. Then you might work your way up as a grip, then a focus puller, and then a camera operator.

Pitfalls

As are most jobs in this industry, crawling up the ladder to become a DOP is incredibly challenging, competitive, and just plain tough. It can take between 10 and 20 years before you really arrive. You'll work very long hours and you'll have to start out on the bottom of the pecking order. It may take years to get to the top.

Perks

This can be a truly glamorous job, with a salary to match! An international director of photography working on big-name movies gets all the perks a director does—international travel, glitzy hotels, paid-for meals, power, and respect—all without having to worry about getting criticized if the movie flops. (That all gets blamed on the director.)

Get a Jump on the Job

You can't start too early to prepare for a career in films. If your family has a DVD or video camera, start making your own films and fiddle around with camera angles and styles. Take any courses you can in high school, or after-school or summer workshops in photography or film. Read books and watch movies too, comparing how different movies are filmed, and how they achieve different effects. Major in film or related studies in college, and try to get internships in related fields over the summer. Keep on doing your own filming.

DOCUMENTARY FILMMAKER

OVERVIEW

Imagine eating every meal—breakfast, lunch, and dinner—at a fast food restaurant for a month, and then filming it. That's what Morgan Spurlock did in the documentary *Super Size Me*, one of the most popular documentaries in recent history. Other documentary filmmakers have gone farther afield to capture their story, lugging film equipment through the jungles of Africa, climbing through the backwoods of Appalachia looking for stories, or shooting the world of circus performers from the inside out. Of course, not all documentary filmmakers put themselves at physical risk, but they're capable of turning out equally impressive movies, such as the films of Ken Burns, so well known for creating documentary classics. If the idea of finding and revealing these nonfiction stories, whether big or small, sounds fascinating, documentary filmmaking might be for you.

So what makes a documentary different from the latest Hollywood blockbuster? A documentary uses film clips and interviews to chronicle actual events with real people. The documentary filmmaker has a very strong opinion and he or she is making the movie to make that point, or reveal an insight. Unlike in Hollywood films, where most of the jobs are union and an electrical expert would never pick up a boom mike, it's much more common for documentary filmmakers to wear many different hats and juggle lots of responsibilities. They may teach, produce, direct, and edit their own work, shoot their own footage, and handle their own sound.

It sounds like a creative person's dream—but don't go reaching for your DVD recorder just yet. What many people don't realize is that a documentary can be just as difficult to make as it is rewarding. Although many documentaries are

AT A GLANCE

Salary Range

$30,000 to $80,000+; can earn $1,000 a day as a freelance documentary camera operator.

Education/Experience

There are no specific training requirements for documentary film producers and directors, although many have either graduated from film school or majored in film or journalism at a liberal arts college. Some experts say you should wait until graduate school to study filmmaking, and should aim for a well-rounded liberal arts education as an undergraduate.

Personal Attributes

Patience, good eye, intelligence, and business acumen are very important.

Requirements

Ability to use a camera, experience, talent, creativity, and professionalism are the factors that are most important in getting many jobs in this industry.

Outlook

Fair; keen competition is expected for the more glamorous jobs. Employment of documentary filmmakers is expected to grow about as fast as the average for all occupations through 2012. Although a growing number of people will aspire to make documentaries, many will leave the field early because the work—when it is available—is hard, the hours are long, and the pay is comparatively low.

produced each year, only a small number of them ever earn much money. Smaller and independent filmmakers often find it difficult to finance new productions, since large motion picture production companies prefer to support established filmmakers. Still, digital technology is lowering production costs for some small-budget films, enabling more independents to succeed in getting their films released nationally. Independent filmmakers will continue to benefit from this technology,

Jan Krawitz, documentary filmmaker

Whether it's a story about the demise of drive-in theaters or life as a dwarf, Jan Krawitz has been independently exploring other realms and other truths by producing and directing documentary films since 1975.

Her most recent film, *Big Enough*, provides an insightful perspective on the world of dwarfism—a follow-up to her earlier film, *Little People*, nominated for an Emmy for Outstanding Individual Documentary. Krawitz's films typically explore diverse subjects, such as a woman's quest for the ideal body (*Mirror Mirror*). *In Harm's Way* is her personal memoir of random violence.

Jan Krawitz didn't begin filming with dreams of winning an Emmy. Instead, she started making movies for her high school graphics arts class with an 8mm camera, exploring social issues popular in the late 60s. By the time she was 15 she was making her own documentaries. "I thought I wanted be a social worker," she recalls, until she fell in love with documentaries during a summer program. She only considered being a documentary filmmaker after realizing she didn't want a career as a social worker. "I didn't feel comfortable in the social work model," she says, "and after watching a couple of documentary films, I realized this was an effective way to expose people to new ideas, new attitudes, and perhaps effect some sort of change or awareness." From then on, she focused on documentary films and filmmaking, getting her master's degree from Temple in documentary film.

After teaching as a graduate assistant at Temple University, she realized she enjoyed teaching, and so for the past 25 years she's taught filmmaking techniques while producing her own documentaries. "It's been a happy marriage, training documentarians and continuing to do my own work," she says. She writes the grants and chooses topics, and then seeks someone to distribute the film. Wearing two hats means she no longer has to work so hard to find money to make the movies she wants to shoot. "The downside is it takes me a long time to make a film," she says. With her last film, she began writing the grant in 1999, and started filming in 2000. By 2005, she was in the throes of distribution.

Some of her students have gone on to create their own documentaries for others, while some work on other people's documentaries and their own at the same time. "There are a lot of people make a living as a documentary filmmaker," she says. "Not like the kind of living a Hollywood director is going to make, but a living."

The biggest hassle is finding the money to fund the projects. "It's frustrating no matter how many you've made, because every time you have to do the whole grant struggle all over again,"

(continues)

because lower costs boost their ability to compete with the major studios

Fortunately, there are many ways to make documentaries without having to raise the money yourself. Some docu-mentarians do corporate work; some get jobs as staff producers for public TV stations; and others work at MTV, *Frontline*, MSNBC, or *National Geographic*, producing documentaries.

(continued)

she says. Still, Krawitz loves the unpredictability of documentary filmmaking. "You set out to do something with a vision and theme, but there is always an unexpected surprise, which is lovely. That doesn't happen as often in a narrative film, which is script-based and not as open as documentaries."

She also loves the creative process of editing. "There's the reality when you set out to make the film, and then there is the reality you have when you come back from the shoot," she explains. "You have to forget what you set out to do, because sometimes what you end up with is different. To me, editing a documentary is an incredibly exciting process. People speak for themselves in a documentary. It's very challenging, to craft a film so the story gets told using the words of the people themselves. In editing I feel like this is the reality, there's no surprises, I know what I have."

Her advice: Don't overshoot just because tape is inexpensive. "Just because it's easy to shoot doesn't mean it's easier to do it well," she says. "Don't assume it's not hard. Everybody makes these way-too-long films. They shoot everything that moves, instead of going out with a concept and shooting carefully. In the past, when you shot with film, you'd better believe it was a considered decision about what to shoot, because film was expensive."

The availability of the digital video has democratized the process, she believes, making filming available to everybody, but she warns that it still requires training. "Our students spend two years learning filmmaking full time, and when they leave they still have tons to learn," she says. "You can read a book about how to make a film, but documentary filmmaking also requires a lot of experience and training."

Instead, you should make sure filmmaking is really what you want to do. "Everyone today is a filmmaker," she says. "I can't tell you how many calls I get, with someone saying: 'I want to make a film, and I'm really inspired. Can you help me?' Today everyone can go out and buy a camera and edit it with iMovie." Instead, she cautions that documentary filmmaking isn't glamorous and fun—it's really just a lot of hard work. "People need to disabuse themselves of the notion that everybody can do it," she says, blaming today's cult of independence. "I heard a guy who bragged that it cost him $260 to do a film about a schizophrenic mother. I think that has perpetuated this notion that anybody can do it, and it doesn't require any training."

Having taken the time to study and learn her craft, to her documentary filmmaking is a passport, an entrée into situations and events to which she would otherwise not have access. Her thesis film *Cotton Candy* gave her the chance of living with a traveling tent circus for a month when she was 25. "It was an interesting, amazing experience," she recalls. "I can't juggle, and I otherwise would never have been there. I got to know them, have the experience of moving to a new town every day. I feel like from a selfish point of view, it's opened me up to all these other worlds that I appreciate. To me that is an exciting thing."

Jobs in the industry can be broadly classified according to the three phases of filmmaking: preproduction, production, and postproduction. Preproduction is the planning phase, which includes budgeting, casting, finding the right location, and scheduling. Next comes production, when you actually make the film. As you shoot your documentary, you may be feeling some stress as you try to meet schedules, stay within budget, and resolve any personnel and production problems while filming on location, often working in adverse weather and under unpleasant and sometimes dangerous conditions. Postproduction takes place in editing rooms and recording studios, where the film is shaped into its final form. Many documentary filmmakers believe that it's in the editing that the true creative process begins, as the footage is cut and shaped to tell a very special, unique story.

Pitfalls

Documentary filmmakers work under constant pressure, and many face stress from the continual need to find their next job. To succeed, they need patience and commitment to their craft. The biggest frustration documentary filmmakers report is the problem of finding people to underwrite their films; grant writing can be difficult and unpredictable, and often a filmmaker begins a project with only partial funding.

Perks

Few things are as creative, freewheeling, and unpredictable as filming a documentary, and if you thrive on these three aspects of a career, you'll have a wonderful time. Filmmakers who have a significant point to make find enormous satisfaction in exploring issues and presenting them in new ways.

Get a Jump on the Job

If you're interested in making documentaries, grab a video or DVD camera and get out there and practice. Study all you can about using your camera, light your subject, and edit your footage. Start out small—one of the big mistakes many amateur documentarians make is to make their films way too long. The more you practice, the better you'll get. Once you're ready to apply to film school, lobby for a grant or funding, or submit one of your longer films to a festival, you'll have had lots of filmmaking practice.

It's also a good idea to learn all you can about digital filmmaking and editing. What with today's computers and editing software, you can get lots of practice making films at home. If you know how to set up your own Web page, you can put your film online and sell it, without having to involve anyone else!

At the same time, study techniques of filmmakers you admire, and take any classes or workshops offered at your school or in your community. One of the best ways to gain this kind of hands-on experience is through internships as a production assistant. You may spend lots of time brewing up coffee and running errands, but you'll also get to see how a documentary is made. Can't find an internship in your area? Call a film school, and read up on some of the school's assigned texts.

FIGHT CHOREOGRAPHER

OVERVIEW

If your heart pounds and your blood thrills to the flash and clang of ancient swordplay, such as the mayhem in movies such as *The Pirates of the Caribbean*, you're probably watching the talented work of fight choreographers—those skilled experts who direct each swoop of the knife or blade in a movie sequence. The performing arts today are quite physical, and audiences demand realism in all forms of entertainment. In fact, stage swordplay is even more demanding before a live audience, because there's no chance at a second take. In a well-choreographed fight scene, you'll be treated to multiple camera angles and sophisticated sound effects so that you can imagine you're right in the middle of the fisticuffs.

There are many different titles for fight choreographer and no one can seem to agree which is preferred, but they include *fight coordinator, fight choreographer, fight arranger, fight director, swordmaster, fencing master, fight consultant*—and the list goes on. Sometimes, choreographers say, the only way to separate yourself from the rest of the fight choreographers is to call yourself by another title—so *fight choreographer* becomes *swordmaster*. But no matter what you call them, their job is to make fight scenes on film or theater look so real you really believe it's spontaneous.

It's hard to say what makes a good fight scene, but most likely you know it when you see it. If a movie calls for a

AT A GLANCE

Salary Range

Salaries of fight choreographers (also known as fight directors) range from less than $5,000 to more than $100,000 a year, depending on how often they work, amount of risk involved, the location of the job, and how widely recognized the choreographer is. Well-known, experienced experts may be able to name their price, while someone just starting out may work for very little, just to gain the experience.

Education/Experience

Many colleges and universities, as well as theaters and private schools, offer high-quality stage combat training associated with an actor training program ranging from a one-semester crash course to a seven-semester overview.

Personal Attributes

Agility, strength, flexibility, physical prowess.

Requirements

Fight choreographers in union films are typically covered under the Screen Actor's Guild.

Outlook

Fair. There isn't a lot of work for fight choreographers, especially with the popularity of computerized visual effects, and the competition is fierce.

sword fight, the director doesn't want to let two A-list actors loose on sound stage, grabbing epées and going at each other. Instead, the director will call in a fight choreographer to pace out every move of the fight sequence—just as if it were a dance routine. The choreographer plans a series of movements step by step, and then teaches the actors how to perform each one. Once each step is mastered, the choreographer teaches the actors how to pull it all together into one smooth routine. Often, the fight choreographer may have to train the actors in the particular type of fighting they're doing.

The Society of American Fight Directors (SAFD) offers a program to train and qualify students to become fight performers, choreographers, and instructors with the SAFD Skills Proficiency Test (formerly known as the Certification Test). The test is offered as a service of the SAFD through its network of certified teachers, fight directors, and fight masters.

Robert Chapin, fight choreographer

To Robert Chapin—actor, musician, writer, special effects wizard, and fight director—choreographing a fight sequence is a lot like dance, "but with a whole lot of adrenaline telling you to duck or jump at the right second!" His specialty is western swordplay—rapier, dagger, and broadsword. But he has also used plenty of other weapons onstage and in films, including the katana, axe, mace, staff, spear, halberd, and good old hand-to-hand and martial arts.

No matter what the method, Chapin figures people know a good fight scene when they see one. "I was 18 at a Renaissance faire back in Miami when I saw the Royal Chessmen perform a choreographed living chess game and I was hooked," he remembers. "There's nothing like seeing a fight sequence performed live.

"The best part of fight choreography is the rush when you finally get a fight sequence up to speed, which can take quite a bit of time if you want to keep it safe," he says. "The worst part of fight choreography is the politics—perhaps even worse than the potential injuries. Much like any other job in the industry, a fight coordinator is subjected to the whims of the director, the rants of the actors, and backstabbing from the competition. I try to tell myself not to take it too seriously."

With 20 years of experience in stage combat, Robert Chapin has choreographed his own fight scenes with some of Hollywood's finest combat choreographers and directors including Steven Spielberg (*Hook*), Mel Brooks (*Robin Hood: Men in Tights*), and Penny Marshall (*Renaissance Man*).

Just like many people in the entertainment business, Chapin is a man of many talents. He initially studied music in college and became an accomplished singer and songwriter, proficient in piano and guitar. Then he discovered the stage, and studied acting, which he continues to pursue. He also trained as a gymnast, stuntman, and horseman.

"I like being able to do a lot of things, and it helps to have something to fall back on," he notes. "There's not a lot of work for fight coordinators—especially those that do swordplay. Most of the swashbuckling films end up shooting overseas where help is cheap and castles are plenty."

Chapin developed his skills in swordplay and stage combat by studying with martial arts masters and attending a variety of formal stage combat training programs, including the Academy of Theatrical Combat in Los Angeles, The Ring of Steel, and Royal Chessmen in Miami. He further honed his skills by performing at Renaissance faires and live shows across the country.

(continues)

Only these qualified members may teach SPT classes and only an SAFD fight master may adjudicate the test.

Although there is no required training to become a fight choreographer in the United States, you can take classes and be certified by the SAFD.

The SAFD also certifies fight choreographer teachers, whose requirements are much different and more difficult than

---

(continued)

Certified with the societies of American, British, and Canadian fight directors, Chapin continues to develop his many skills, working behind the camera as second unit director and writer. In addition to his other talents, Robert holds a B.S. in computer science, and often works as a visual effects artist; he's created effects for feature films including *American Beauty*, *Armageddon*, and *Crouching Tiger, Hidden Dragon*.

"Wearing many hats has helped me on numerous occasions," he observes. "Everything adds to your marketability. The fact that I can write, direct, edit, and supervise visual effects has come in quite handy. It's even pulled me out of a few tight spots when I've needed to use visual effects or camera tricks to enhance an action sequence."

His advice to fight choreographer wannabes: Make your own work! "When I first came to LA, I realized that there wasn't much of a chance in landing a starring role as a swordsman," he says, "so I took the initiative and wrote a script. *Ring of Steel* was produced a year later by MCA/Universal for $1.5 million." But even if you don't have a lot of money, you can still create your own work, he says. "I began an Internet series several years ago called *The Hunted* [http://www.thehunted.tv], which began as a no-budget class project. I've produced over 16 short episodes so far and it's been a great experience for myself and my students."

He tells kids interested in fighting and swordplay to check out the Renaissance fairs. "They're a great place to learn all this stuff," he says. "A lot of other coordinators I know got their start there. I performed for three years in Miami with the Royal Chessmen, two years with a jousting troupe, another two years with a group called Ring of Steel, and several years in Southern California directing and performing in touring shows such as The Fighting Chessmen and Fyne Arte of Wenching."

At the moment, he's highly marketable because there aren't any other fight coordinators—at least that he knows of—who are also visual effects artists. "Many stuntmen and fight choreographers feel threatened that they might be replaced by visual effects," he says, "but I understand that computer graphics are just another tool—like a ratchet or an airbag. It's just one more thing to add to your bag of tricks—and it's a darn cool trick with virtually no limitations!"

It's a business that's endlessly interesting to him. "There are folks who take credit for fight choreography when a lot of what they do is to take a couple fighters and tell them to work up a fight. I would call that a fight coordinator. I've choreographed most of my own fights for major feature films without receiving any credit, but that's just part of the job. Learn from everyone you can. There are many different styles out there and there is no one person that has all the answers. Just remember to play safe."

those in the performance track (actor/combatant, advanced actor/combatant) and must demonstrate a lifelong commitment to polishing these skills.

Pitfalls

Working on a movie set surrounded by large egos and lots of creativity can be challenging; as with many areas of entertainment jobs, it's also difficult to break into this field.

Perks

Done well, fight choreography is a graceful, athletic art requiring split-second timing and great strength and control. Doing it well can be enormously satisfying and financially lucrative, once you get well known and established.

Get a Jump on the Job

If you think there's nothing more fun than swashbuckling, check out a Renaissance faire near your home—almost every state has them, typically running from June through October. Renaissance faires feature a lot of swordplay, jousting, and other types of martial arts, and they're a great way to break in. Then start taking classes offered by the SAFD in your town.

FOCUS PULLER

OVERVIEW

Who'd want to watch a film in which the action was fuzzy and out of focus? Nobody—which is why the job of a focus puller is so important in the entertainment industry. Pulling focus is the process of changing the focus setting of the camera lens as the action on the set changes, which allows the camera operator to keep the scene in focus. It's just one of the jobs of a focus puller, along with various other responsibilities such as setting up cameras; selecting, mounting, and changing lenses; and keeping lenses clean for the camera operator. A focus puller's more common name is the somewhat less glamorous *camera assistant*.

It's the responsibility of the focus puller to remain with the camera as it's moved around the set. He or she often will work with other crew members to keep track of the details of each camera shot, and get ideas for camera angles.

A focus puller's day begins early, before the camera operator gets to the set, because it's the focus puller's job to get the cameras set up and ready to go for the camera operator. On some sets, the focus puller also is expected to perform other more mundane tasks, such as fetching coffee.

On the photography pecking order, the position of focus puller is about midway up the ladder. If you're interested in cameras, you'd normally start as a runner, progress to a clapper loader, move into focus puller, and then become

AT A GLANCE

Salary Range

Salaries for focus pullers vary widely, depending on the employer and circumstances of the production. Many focus pullers are self-employed, and may be paid by the project or on a daily basis. The average yearly salary for a focus puller is between $32,000 and $35,000, although those with union memberships often can earn more.

Education/Experience

While there are no specific educational requirements to be a focus puller, many in the job have degrees from art or film schools. A photography course at a vocational school also could be helpful, and some film schools offer intensive short-term courses or workshops for people who want to concentrate in a specific area of the entertainment industry. Some formal training is almost always necessary to get a job as a focus puller.

Personal Attributes

Must have good technical and artistic abilities, and be able to work as part of a team and to remain cool under pressure. You'll need to be able to stay focused and maintain total concentration for long periods of time. You also should have a reasonable level of physical fitness, because you may be required to stand for long periods and work long days.

Requirements

Prior work is highly valued, so you might have to start out in a position other than focus puller to gain some on-the-job experience. Some aspiring focus pullers even start out as runners in order to get on a film set. Some employers require membership in an entertainment industry union.

Outlook

Jobs in the entertainment industry, including focus puller, are expected to increase by between 10 and 20 percent through the year 2012. That job growth is considered to be average, according to government statistics.

a camera operator, lighting cameraperson, and finally director of photography. It can take many years to reach all the way to the top of the photographic heap, to occupy the dizzying position of director of photography.

There are two ways to train to become a focus puller. Some people think it's helpful to get some on-the-job training and then go to a film school or other school that offers camera training. Others insist it's better to do the schooling first, and then get on-the-job experience. If you look for on-the-job training before going to school, you're likely to have to work for very little or no pay. If you choose that route, you should probably think of the work as free education.

Pitfalls

Being a focus puller is physically demanding, and often requires that you stay on your feet for hours at a time. Because it's the job of a focus puller to set up cameras before filming begins and to take them down afterwards, you can count on some very long days during filming. Since movie making doesn't always happen during banker's hours (from 9 a.m. to 5 p.m.),

Franco Miro, focus puller

Franco (short for Francisco) Miro grew up in Barcelona, but during the 10 years that he's been working as a focus puller, he's had the opportunity to travel extensively, including many jobs in the United States. That's one of the secrets to success in that job, he says: Make yourself available to be considered for as many jobs as possible. "Even if you don't leave your own country, you'll probably need to travel within your country," Miro says.

Like most focus pullers, Miro must keep the action being filmed in focus, as well as maintain the cameras before, during, and after filming. He must know exactly what lenses will be necessary and where they are, so that the filming can proceed smoothly. "I also set up the cameras at the beginning of the day and strike them at the end," Miro says. "There's no such thing as a short day when you're filming."

Miro says he works with the script supervisor during shooting so he can keep up-to-date with the details of each shot. Every shot is different, he says, and you have to be sure you understand the expectations for each.

Miro, who has a B.A. in film studies from Canterbury Christ Church University College in Kent, England, speaks fluent English as well as Spanish. Because communication between crew members is very important, it's obviously impossible to work in a location where you don't know the language.

The job of a focus puller can be very stressful, Miro says. You're expected to pretty much stay attached to the camera during the entire filming process, which is tiring and can be exasperating. "The work is tedious and there is a lot of pressure on you," Miro says.

He advises anyone interested in becoming a focus puller to get some education. Although you may have to take low-paying jobs at first, he warns, don't be afraid to work hard, and you'll be successful in this job.

you'll probably be working nights and weekends when shooting is underway.

Perks

When you're working as a focus puller, you're right where the action is, which can give you exposure and access to big-time directors, actors, and producers. Working as a focus puller also will give you a first-hand look at other aspects of photography and puts you in a position to advance your career.

Get a Jump on the Job

Begin by learning everything you can about photography. Your high school may offer a photography course, or you could enroll in a photography program at a vocational-technical school. Many community colleges offer non-credit programs, including photography. Some schools have clubs in which students are involved with photography and filming. If your school doesn't have such a club, you could ask about forming one. Once you get to college, start taking every film or camera course you can, and see if you can take some internships over the summer for more experience.

LOCATION SCOUT

OVERVIEW

Did you ever wonder how film directors find those exotic beaches that you see in movies? Or where car manufacturers locate those long stretches of beautiful roadway that you see in car commercials? Just as in the real estate business, a big part of Hollywood's success is location, location, location. Would *CSI: Miami* have the same appeal if it was filmed in Ohio or Arkansas? Or if *The OC* was set in New Jersey? Not a chance. And the person responsible for finding the perfect setting for a movie, TV show, or commercial—sometimes with only a cloudy concept of what the director has in mind—is the location scout.

A location scout looking for the perfect place to film a movie or TV show normally is given a script, which suggests all the locations that will be necessary for filming. The location scout works with the director and production designer to decide what sort of look they all want—and then he or she goes out and finds it. Locations are identified either by traveling to different areas or going through files of location photos, or a combination of the two. Once an appropriate location has been located, the scout will photograph it and take the photos back to the director for approval.

Think about some movies and TV shows you've seen recently, and you'll start to get an appreciation for how difficult a location scout's job can be. Finding the perfect spot to film a movie about people trapped in the woods after their

AT A GLANCE

Salary Range

An experienced location scout working on a major project on a freelance basis can earn between $400 and $1,200 a day, depending on the type of job, location, risk involved, travel required, and other factors. Smaller projects usually pay between $200 and $400 a day. Location scouts who work in-house with a production company or corporation can expect to earn between $40,000 and $70,000 a year, depending on experience and job responsibility.

Education/Experience

Although there are no firm educational requirements to be a location scout, most employers will expect at least a bachelor's degree in film, fine arts, or a related field. Most employers will want you to have completed at least one internship, as well.

Personal Attributes

You should be able to get along with people and work as part of a team, be resourceful and creative, punctual, responsible, and willing to see a project through once you begin it. You should have skills necessary to convince people to work with you, be able to clearly communicate ideas and information, and have an eye for detail.

Requirements

Reliable transportation and a valid driver's license. You should have a good sense of geography and direction, and thorough knowledge of the area in which you'll be scouting. Union membership may be required for some jobs and photography skills are necessary.

Outlook

Jobs in the entertainment industry, including those for location scouts, are expected to increase by between 10 and 20 percent through the year 2012. That job growth is considered to be average.

plane crashes isn't always a walk in the park. Often, a location scout is expected to find an area nearby in which to film that looks like someplace in a completely different location. The TV show *Roswell*, for instance, is supposed to take place in Roswell, New Mexico, but is actually filmed in Covina, California.

Location scouts must find houses that look like they're haunted, cemeteries in which to film funerals, churches in which to film weddings, perfect beaches, mountaintop retreats, unspoiled stretches of roadway, and a myriad of other settings. They do this by either actually going out and looking for them, or going through

Kevin Murphy, San Diego location scout

Kevin Murphy has scouted locations for all kinds of film or print. He's scouted locations for television productions, magazine and catalog shoots, music videos, and small film projects. He also serves as a location manager on many jobs, and keeps up a photography business on the side.

Murphy has a photography background and worked for a time as a tour guide, primarily in the Sierra Mountains of California. In that job, he got to know his way around the region and met a lot of forest rangers and other personnel. When he gave up the tour guide business, he got back into camera work and worked several jobs in the Sierra Mountain region. While there, he realized that he had credentials as a location scout because he knew so much about the area and had many contacts there. One thing led to another, and soon he was scouting locations.

More than a decade later, Murphy takes on mostly commercial scouting work because it pays better and generally doesn't involve the extensive travel often required with a movie or TV shoot. His specialty, he says, is scouting for car commercials. "I know where to find some really nice roads," he says.

While Murphy enjoys going out and looking for the perfect location, he also finds great satisfaction in turning someone's idea of a location into a real place. Basically, he says, finding the right location is a matter of knowing where to look. "You take an idea or a concept and then you put together a plan of where you're going to go and how you're going to find the place you want," Murphy says. "It's pretty much just going out and finding things."

Murphy, who generally charges between $400 and $1,200 a day depending on the job profile, advises anyone interested in being a location scout to earn a bachelor's degree in an area such as commercial art, theater arts, or fine arts. Then go out and find an internship and/or an entry-level job in the entertainment industry in order to get some experience. "I think that you need a college degree these days for almost every job in the business," he says. "It just sort of sets you up for life, you know? But what an employer is really going to look for is some hands-on experience."

A job as an assistant in a production house, camera rental shop, editing house, or commercial agency will teach you a lot about the industry and give you some credentials when you start looking for a job, Murphy says. "Too many people try to just hang out their shingle when they've never done anything before," he says. "Hands-on experience in a working environment is just invaluable."

file after file of photos of various locations. While the job can be fun, it also can be challenging.

Many location scouts also work as location managers, which means their jobs entail much more than just finding a place to film a movie, TV show, or commercial. They need to find out who owns the property if it is private and secure permission to use it; contact municipal officials about using public property; work with police, park rangers, caretakers, and property owners; and generally attend to a whole lot of details, such as where the filming crew can eat. Details, as you probably know, can easily turn into hassles. A location manager may have to secure the rights to film in Yankee Stadium, Yellowstone National Park, on a college campus, or in a private citizen's house. Sometimes that's easy to do, but other times it's incredibly challenging.

Most location scouts start out as a production assistant or some other entry level position with a production house and work their way up in the industry. Others come into the field from a photography background. Once a location scout has acquired a good deal of experience and has gained a reputation, he or she usually moves into more commercial work, leaving movie and TV scouting to those with less experience and influence. That's because commercial scouting generally pays better and doesn't entail the long days in sometimes tedious conditions that film and TV work can.

Pitfalls

As with almost any area of show business, it can be difficult to break into the field of location scouting. Competition can be fierce, especially for those without a lot of experience. You might have to take on some low paying, generally undesirable jobs before you've built up enough experience and reputation to move up.

Perks

Location scouting is really the act of turning a concept—and idea—into a reality. You're taking a vision and making it happen, which can be very rewarding. As a location scout you'll get to travel, meet many people, and be involved with the process of filming a movie, show, or commercial. Once you're established, you can choose the jobs you want and make some nice money.

Get a Jump on the Job

Photography skills are important for a location scout, so if you're not already into photography, you should sign up for a course or at least get some books or videos to help you get started. If possible, get a job in a camera shop. Study the geography of the area in which you hope to work and learn your way around.

MOTIVATIONAL SPEAKER

OVERVIEW

Motivational speakers come in all shapes and sizes, from all backgrounds, and with many levels of education and experience. The one thing all successful speakers have in common, however, is their ability to engage an audience. You might get hired once, but if you fail to present a speech that grabs the attention and imagination of your audience, chances are slim that you'll be invited back.

It is the job of a motivational speaker to motivate, but subject matter varies tremendously from person to person. One motivational speaker, for instance, may talk about staying hopeful while recovering from a life-threatening illness, while another might motivate business executives to build more effective and efficient management teams. You can hire motivational speakers to talk about business issues, women's issues, diversity issues, communication issues, team-building, sports and adventure, personal challenge—the list goes on and on.

There's a vast range of potential topics. The trick is to find a topic that interests you, and then to become an expert on all aspects. You can't, for example, speak convincingly about surviving a life-threatening illness if you've never had one. You can't effectively discuss climbing Mt. Everest if you've never topped anything higher than the hill in your backyard. And you can't motivate a business executive to squeeze more productivity out of her workers if you don't fully understand

AT A GLANCE

Salary Range

A beginning professional motivational speaker might earn between $1,500 and $3,000 per speech. More experienced speakers generally earn between $3,500 and $12,500 per speech, while celebrity speakers can earn between $15,000 and $115,000 per speech. However, it's extremely difficult to estimate a salary range for a motivational speaker, because it depends on how often the person speaks, his or her experience, credentials, and how well he or she is known.

Education/Experience

A motivational speaker must be extremely knowledgeable in one or more areas in order to have something to talk about with authority. At least a bachelor's degree in business, education, or another applicable field is highly recommended.

Personal Attributes

Should be comfortable with the idea of speaking in front of many people; be able to talk comfortably and authoritatively about the topics in which you specialize; appear neat and well groomed. A pleasant speaking voice also is a plus, although people with distinctive voices also have been successful.

Requirements

You don't need to be affiliated with a speaker's bureau or organization in order to be a motivational speaker, but your credentials will be much better, and you'll have more chance for national recognition if you are. Many professional motivational speakers are members of the National Speaker's Association, or they are represented by a speaker's bureau, such as the Minneapolis-based Preferred Speakers or the Santa Barbara-based Big Speak.

Outlook

The availability of motivational speaking jobs varies depending on the state of business and the

(continues)

AT A GLANCE (*continued*)

economy in general, job growth predictions, and other factors. Overall, motivational speaking jobs are expected to increase by between 10 and 20 percent through the year 2012. That job growth is considered to be average.

the person's business and the people who work there.

Motivational speakers (except for celebrities who become speakers based on their fame) typically must work their way up the speaking ladder, honing their skills, confidence, and presentation abilities as they go along. Most speakers begin by picking a topic they'd like to talk about, and then learning everything they can about the subject. If you decided you're going to speak on managing stress, for instance, you'd need to become an expert in the areas of stress and stress management. While you probably wouldn't need to go to medical school to accomplish that, you'd certainly need to conduct extensive research and have a high degree of medical knowledge.

Nearly all motivational speakers start out locally, speaking to groups at churches or synagogues, civic organizations, schools, or other locations where people gather. Often, these jobs are low paying, or unpaid, but provide invaluable experience.

Many people offer (or are asked) to speak about their jobs or careers, especially if the job is not one that is well known. A pest control operator might speak about common household pests and how to control them, or a prison chaplain talk about life in a prison and the inmates

she has counseled. As long as you're thoroughly acquainted with your topic, with proper skill and technique you can make just about any topic interesting and inspiring.

Perhaps the most basic and important rule about public speaking is to never attempt to talk about something you don't know. If you're not an expert on stress management, all you're going to do is raise everyone's stress level by trying to talk about it.

Once you've built up a local reputation as a good speaker, jobs are likely to find you. Or, you can begin advertising your services in area or regional publications. There is always a demand for speakers, and individuals and groups are willing to pay to meet those demands.

Pitfalls

Until you're well established as a motivational speaker, it may be very difficult to make a living. Many speakers give talks on the side while holding down full-time jobs. Because motivational speaking at a professional level can require a lot of travel, your work might force you to spend a lot of time away from home, which is difficult for many people.

Perks

Well-known motivational speakers can command high salaries and perks, such as stays in fancy hotels and first-class air travel. If you enjoy being in the spotlight, there may be no better job for you than that of a motivational speaker. When you're in front of an audience of 2,000 people—it's all about you and what you say.

Lenora Billings-Harris, motivational speaker

Lenora Billings-Harris didn't set out to be a public speaker. Her career, as she says, "just sort of happened." Currently, she owns Excel Development Systems, Inc. in Greensboro, North Carolina, and is vice president and president-elect of the National Speakers Association.

With an undergraduate degree in education and a master's degree in adult education, Billings-Harris first came in contact with public speakers while developing and directing seminars at the University of Michigan. "My job entailed hiring professional speakers," she says. "They came there from all over the world."

That position led to one with the General Motors Corporation, in which she planned and conducted management seminars for GM auto dealers. Billings-Harris loved teaching the seminars, and found that speaking in front of a group of people was exhilarating and challenging. "I realized I was definitely doing what I loved," she says.

In 1986 Billings-Harris, who is now 54, started her own company to develop and conduct training programs for business and industry. While she was talking in front of groups, she still didn't think of herself as a public speaker. "At that point, I still thought that doing this business was to go out and do training programs," she says.

Many people who heard Billings-Harris speak were very impressed, and some recommended that she join the National Speakers Association. She did so, and by joining, she opened up all sorts of new doors for herself. "Then I realized there was this whole world of speakers that I had not been aware of before," she says.

Billings-Harris began seriously contemplating life as a motivational speaker. The challenge, she learned, would be to narrow down her subject matter to a deliverable and arresting topic. "I really liked doing it all, but I knew I had to narrow it down," she says. "There was this buzzword called 'diversity' back in the late 1980s, and I recognized it as a new field."

Support from her peers kept her encouraged as she debated whether or not to focus on the issue of diversity. A trip to South Africa in the early 1990s confirmed her decision to become a speaker who specialized in topics dealing with diversity.

Today, Billings-Harris estimates she accepts 75 to 100 speaking engagements each year, ranging from keynote speeches to three-day training seminars. "I'm on the road about 50 to 60 percent of the time," she says.

The training seminars Billings-Harris conducts tend to be for corporations, she says, while keynote speeches normally are presented to professional organizations. Her lengthy client list

Get a Jump on the Job

Get involved in any sort of school activity that will put you in front of others, such as a speech class, debate club, or a Model United Nations club. If you do something that others might find interesting, offer to talk about it. If you spend two weeks of your summer vacation building homes with Habitat for Humanity, for instance, a civic or religious group probably would be glad for you to come in and talk about your experience in front of a group. When you get to be 18, consider joining a local chapter of Toastmasters International, a group that promotes public speakers and holds training and meetings all over the country.

includes Comcast Cable Communications, Domino's Pizza, the American Heart Association, American Express, AT&T, General Motors Corp., Texaco/Shell, University of North Carolina, Cornell University, National Association of Women Business Owners, National Education Association, and the Dallas Chamber of Commerce.

She works with 15 to 20 different speaker's bureaus, which refer clients who are looking to address diversity issues. She also has an extensive Web site and has written a book exploring diversity-related issues. The most effective advertising she does, however, is to appeal to every audience to which she speaks.

"My primary means of advertising is to do the very best I can every time I get in front of an audience," Billings-Harris says. "There are human beings in every audience, and every human being is connected to 250 other human beings, at least."

In other words, word of mouth is key to being a successful speaker.

Billings-Harris does not remember ever feeling uncomfortable speaking in front of a group. She acknowledges, however, that for most people, public speaking is very intimidating. "Actually, it (public speaking) is the number one fear, greater even than death," she says.

If you are not entirely comfortable speaking in front of a group of people at this point, Billings-Harris advises you not to worry, but to keep working to increase your comfort level.

You can do that, she says, by joining any sort of group or taking advantage of any opportunity that gets you in front of other people, such as presenting themes, participating in plays, joining debate or other clubs, or volunteering to read in a religious setting. The most important educational consideration, she advised, is to study something in which you are very, very interested, and learn everything you can about the subject.

"Major in something that you really love," she says. "And then get speaking experience in whatever way you can." That may include joining a local chapter of Toastmasters International or volunteering to speak to civic groups, religious groups, or school groups.

"Learn your topic well, and develop a speech that's compelling," Billings-Harris says. "Then, just do it constantly. And what happens is that, after a while, somebody comes up and asks if you can speak to their group and how much you'll charge to do so. And then you'll be a professional speaker."

OPERA SINGER

OVERVIEW

When you think of an opera singer, you probably imagine a person who sings classical music in a foreign language at a very high range. But there's actually quite a lot more to the job than that. Opera singers perform in a type of theatrical production set to music, which they must interpret using their knowledge of voice production, melody, and harmony to sing character parts or perform in their own individual style. Singers are typically classified according to their voice range—soprano, contralto, tenor, baritone, or bass.

To become an opera singer, you've got to spend years training your voice with private teachers. Most study at music conservatories or major in voice at a university. University training is also valuable because you'll be given lots of chances to perform that you might not be able to find anywhere else. The choice of teacher is important, because if you don't study with an authentic teacher, you'll never sound authentic yourself. You also study languages—you should be fluent in five or six so that you can sing in a variety of tongues. After years of training, you may begin singing small roles on stage. When you do begin to perform, you may sing in the chorus of an opera, eventually earning a support role and finally reaching the upper echelon of the opera world: a principal singer. In the beginning, you may be a "house singer" with an opera company (singers who remain with the company) such as the Metropolitan

AT A GLANCE

Salary Range
$40,000 to $250,000+ a year.

Education/Experience
Music training at a conservatory or university, and/or private vocal lessons. The National Association of Schools of Music accredits nearly 600 college-level programs in music. Courses typically include musical theory, music interpretation, composition, conducting, and performance in a particular instrument or in voice.

Personal Attributes
Willingness to take risks, and patience. Opera singers always must make their performances look effortless; therefore, preparation and practice are important. They also must be prepared to face the anxiety of intermittent employment and of rejection when auditioning.

Requirements
Musical talent, versatility, creativity, poise, and a good stage presence. Because quality performance requires constant study and practice, self-discipline is vital.

Outlook
Fair. Competition for jobs for singers is expected to be keen, and there are far more people who want to perform than there are openings. Talent alone is no guarantee of success; many people start out to become an opera star, but leave the profession because they find the work difficult, the discipline demanding, and the long periods of intermittent unemployment unendurable. Overall employment of opera singers is expected to grow about as fast as the average for all occupations through 2012.

Opera in New York City. Eventually, most opera singers want to reach a point where they're not just singing in one house, but are traveling to a number of different companies all over the world, so they can become well known, such as Pavarotti or Beverly Sills. Moreover, opera singers don't necessarily want to give their life over to just one company; those who do stay with one company to make it easier on their family life, because they want absolute security, and to have insurance and benefits.

In many ways, opera singers are a bit like actors, having to audition for singing roles and win the chance to perform better and better roles as they gain more experi-

---

Elizabeth Printy, soprano opera singer

When Elizabeth Printy was about 10 years old, she stumbled on a set of old classical recordings sitting by a trash can. "I dragged them home, and that's when I first heard Beethoven's Fifth, and the music of *Swan Lake*, and the recordings of Eileen Farrell, one of the great American opera singers," she says. Those initial old records piqued her curiosity for classical music, and within five years she began singing in a choir and chorus.

But it took a recording of Maria Callas singing *Lucia di Lammermoor*, to get Printy really hooked. "She was the greatest Lucia, the greatest Tosca ever," Printy says. "Not only did she have an amazing voice, but she threw the drama into it. You could hear these emotions as she would sing." Printy started to sing along with the recording of Lucia, making up her own Italian, mimicking what she thought she heard. "It was my own adulterated version of Lucia in French, Polish, and Italian," Printy laughs. "With that music, if you practice it, you start to stretch your voice, and you sing in realms you never thought you could achieve. You start singing up in the stratosphere. It was very inspiring."

By age 16, realizing that she could probably do a lot more with her voice, Printy honed her talent with a successful voice teacher whose students had gone on to sing at the Met. After high school, she moved on to the New England Conservatory of Music in Boston, to study piano and voice. After graduation came the long years an opera singer must wait until the voice matures. "It's very, very unusual for singers to be able to segue right into singing positions after they graduate from college," she explains. "With singing it takes a much longer time to develop the instrument fully than it does for a pianist or violinist." Such musicians can reach their peak in their teens or 20s, whereas a singer has to physically wait for all the apparatus to develop—often not until their 30s.

"It's almost as if you must wait until your body has reached its full realized musical form," she says, "before you can make such an impression. You can be in your 20s and show promise and people can keep their eye on you, but it's very unusual that someone can achieve a position of stardom at that age."

Most singers take temporary jobs to make sure they will be free to audition at a moment's notice. "When I got out of college I worked for I. Magnin, Bonwit Teller," Printy says. "I just did jobs that didn't get in my way of what I really wanted to do. I would run to Chicago to audition or to New York City. For every 10 auditions, if you got one job, you feel like you're victorious."

By age 24, Printy began winning competitions and auditions and was eventually invited to come sing at the Aldeburgh Festival in England.

(continues)

(continued)

That put her on the operatic map, but her first real professional break came when she sang as an apprentice at Wolf Trap in Virginia. First singing supporting roles, she eventually starred in *The Medium*. "From that point, I was given more roles by different companies," she says.

Since then, Printy's brilliant soprano has thrilled audiences at opera houses throughout the world; she has sung principal roles at the Metropolitan Opera, the Boston Lyric Opera, the New York City Opera, the Opera Theatre of St. Louis, and the Greater Miami Opera. She's also appeared on TV, performing at the Kennedy Center gala honoring fellow opera diva Beverly Sills.

Although she could have opted for the security of remaining with just one company as a house singer, Printy chose to travel to opera companies all around the world. "If you're willing to take a risk and you're successful," she says, "it can be much more rewarding. You travel the world, and you probably get to do a lot more professionally because you go after roles as opposed to being given something."

When she travels to an opera company, it could be for a brief, two-week period or for a month or two. "Usually you've got to give yourself at least three weeks of rehearsal to create a really solid production," she says. Because her time was limited, on longer engagements her husband and daughter would come to visit for a few days on location.

Printy advises young singers to prepare well. "Sometimes singers try to get out there and do it before their voices are really ready," she says. "They want to skimp on training and they don't want the hard work and to take the time to hone their instrument."

Later on, she explains, "The voice suffers if it hasn't been toughened for the job. Lots of singers will fall by the wayside. Many jobs I collected because someone didn't take care of herself." She also recommends that students prepare themselves by learning the history of the opera. "You can't go onstage and sing the role if you don't know anything about the character, the history, the mode of dress or how they walked, what society was like at that time," she says. "You can't play a Mozart heroine and not know how to wear empire dresses and walk as if you're walking on air. It takes practice.

"You need to know every word you're saying in the language, and you need to know every word others are saying that includes you. If someone is saying 'I love you' and you look at them blankly, you've failed dramatically."

As her career has evolved, she has reached the point where she can choose her roles. "I love going to different countries," she says, "visiting all the different states, having the time off to visit museums. I love sampling different foods, and I love the parties the patron throws.

"A lot of people love to sing," she says. "If they would not limit themselves to only listening to one kind of music, they might find that there's a lot more out there they might want to learn about. Here I was in my teens and most of my friends were listening to the Beatles and the Stones and I was listening to Maria Callas. It was kind of a lonely road, but I was never sorry for it."

ence. Some opera singers have agents, who handle the person's schedule, negotiate contracts, locate jobs, and provide information about auditions and set them up. Once you get an opera part, you need to spend lots of time researching your role and then rehearsing it with the company. During rehearsal, you'll learn your part and also the staging of the production, and you'll be fitted for costumes.

Although opera singers don't reach their peak until their 30s (and some take even longer), they can continue to sing into their 70s if they have taken care of their voice, resting it in between performances and singing correctly.

Pitfalls

Breaking in takes as much time in opera as it does in other forms of entertainment—and maybe longer. It can take as much as 10 years after you graduate before you'll be getting good roles, because that's how long it takes for your voice to mature. There can be a lot of traveling and competition.

Perks

If you were born to sing, nothing can compare to standing on stage and letting your voice perform fine music. The salary for accomplished opera singers is attractive, and successful singers can travel the world to sing at great opera houses.

Get a Jump on the Job

If you love to sing, take lessons from a vocal teacher—but follow your teacher's recommendations. Young singers can ruin their voices by singing incorrectly or straining their voice. Listen to lots of excellent classical music, and visit operas whenever possible to hear live opera singers.

ORCHESTRA CONDUCTOR

OVERVIEW

Close your eyes for a moment and think about listening to beautifully performed music. Imagine you're hearing strings mixing with brass and woodwinds. You hear keyboards in the background, mingling with the sounds of percussion instruments. As important as the musicians and instruments are to an orchestra, it is the conductor who puts all the sounds together and weaves the tapestry of music.

The conductor directs the rehearsals and performances of the orchestra, transferring his or her musical interpretations of each piece of music to the members of the orchestra. Conductors also direct other musical groups, such as bands, opera companies, and choruses. Many conductors also serve as musical directors of their orchestras or other musical groups, which means they're responsible for keeping the orginization fully staffed and choosing musical programs.

At first glance, you might think that conducting an orchestra would be simple, but if you study an accomplished conductor you'll soon notice there are many tasks to be carried out. For the conductor to assure that all musicians will begin playing at the appropriate time and stay together during the piece, he or she opens the piece by beating time. This sets the tempo of the music for the musicians. The conductor maintains precise rhythm throughout the piece by signaling to musicians with nods, hand motions, or looks. He or she also uses motions to indicate musical

AT A GLANCE

Salary Range

The salaries of orchestra conductors vary greatly, depending on the size of the orchestra, its location, and other factors. The U.S. Bureau of Labor Statistics reports a median salary of $31,310, with the middle 50 percent earning between $23,820 and $46,350. Conductors of large, metropolitan orchestras, however, earn much more.

Education/Experience

You will need a bachelor's degree in music, and, depending on the size and scope of the orchestra, a master's or doctorate in music. You also will need to have extensive musical training.

Personal Attributes

In addition to exceptional musical talent, an orchestra conductor must have the ability to connect with and inspire musicians, and to impart an understanding of his or her musical style to orchestra members. You should be dedicated to and passionate about music, and have overall knowledge and appreciation of the arts in general.

Requirements

Mastery of at least one musical instrument and a thorough understanding of the workings of all musical instruments. The ability to hear more than one musical part at a time (called *ear training*) is necessary, as is experience in musical composition, mastery of different musical styles, and an understanding of different musical periods. You will need to know standard conducting methods, and should have exceptional skills in musical analysis. Knowledge of French, German, and Italian—the languages of the greatest composers—is recommended.

Outlook

The number of orchestra conductor jobs is expected to increase by between 10 and 20 percent through the year 2012. That job growth is considered to be average.

volume, emphasis, balance, and phrasing. Ultimately, the conductor is responsible for the quality of sound the musicians produce. He or she must ensure that the group of individuals who make up the orchestra become a cohesive and unified sound.

Most of the work of a conductor, however, is performed out of sight of the public eye. Conductors spend long periods of time studying each piece of music before the orchestra even begins to practice it. The conductor must fully know and understand the music in order to formulate his or her interpretation of the work. This requires musical intelligence and confidence. Once the conductor has interpreted the music and has a clear idea of how he or she wants the piece to sound, the conductor must be able to convey that vision to the musicians. Conductors also must have strong stage presence and flair for performing.

All musical endeavors require some training, but conducting requires many years of musical training, schooling, and experience. Conductors should be masters of at least one musical instrument, and accomplished in several others. An

Donald Spieth, orchestra conductor

Donald Spieth is humbled when he conducts musical works written by composers such as Beethoven, Bach, Tchaikovsky, Mendelssohn, or Vivaldi. He feels a great responsibility to interpret the music and conduct it as the composers intended for it to be played.

"I'm just a vessel so that their music can be played," says Spieth, of Allentown, Pennsylvania. "I'm an interpreter for the composer to the orchestra."

Spieth's musical career began like so many other musical careers—at a very young age, when he started playing trumpet with the fourth grade band. As his musical interests grew, so did his knowledge and ability to play different instruments. He soon knew that he wanted to major in music when he went to college, and, shortly after he enrolled as a music major at the University of Iowa, he decided that he would be an orchestra conductor. "When I got to the university and played in my first orchestra, I decided that's what I wanted to do—be an orchestra conductor," Spieth says.

He earned undergraduate and graduate degrees in music performance and literature, then landed his first job as an orchestra conductor with a small college in Pennsylvania. A series of jobs with small, community orchestras led him eventually to the Lehigh Valley Chamber Orchestra, an ensemble of about 40 members. He also still conducts a smaller, community orchestra, and teaches a limited number of music lessons at an area community college.

"I feel very fortunate to have been able to do the things I've done in this field," Spieth says. Although his primary job and first love is the chamber orchestra, Spieth says it is not atypical for an orchestra conductor to hold more than one job, sometimes in completely different fields. Competition for conducting jobs is keen, and supplementing the conductor's salary often is necessary. "I was told once by an agent that if I would resign from my job tomorrow, there would be 400 applications for it," he says.

(continues)

excellent understanding of music theory, history, and style also is necessary.

If you love music and your dream is to be a conductor, you'll need to be disciplined and dedicated, willing to undertake many years of schooling, and devoted to learning everything you can about music, instruments, and sound. With adequate talent and the proper training, instinct, and determination, there's no telling how far you could go—you could even end up onstage at New York City's Metropolitan Opera.

Pitfalls

Positions conducting large, prestigious orchestras are limited, so if that's your dream, you may have to adjust your sights until you're fully established. Some conducting jobs involve a lot of travel, which can pose difficulties. Unless you get

(continued)

All orchestras have different practice and performance schedules, so there's no such thing as a typical schedule for a conductor. Because the Lehigh Valley Chamber Orchestra includes professional musicians from a wide geographical area, including New York City, Philadelphia, and the Allentown, Pennsylvania, area, it condenses its practices and concerts into four days.

Concerts are held about once a month beginning in September and continuing through May. On concert weeks, the orchestra practices for two and a half hours Wednesday night, and for five hours on Thursday afternoon and night. There is another rehearsal on Friday afternoon, and performances Friday and Saturday nights.

"It's a very compressed schedule," Spieth says. "But we've found it works the best for us because so many of our musicians have to travel."

The orchestra also presents family shows, school concerts, and other performances and events.

On non-concert weeks, Spieth concentrates on learning and interpreting the music. By the time the orchestra convenes to practice, he has a clear idea in his mind of how the piece should sound.

Spieth advises aspiring conductors to get experience on a number of musical instruments, including a keyboard. And, he says, join as many musical groups as you have time for. "Playing music with other people is very valuable experience," Spieth says. "Play in as many ensembles as you can."

He warns that being an orchestra conductor is hard work—physically, mentally, and emotionally. "Music has to move you, and you need to be able to express that to the audience," Spieth says. "But it's not only an emotional attachment, it's a physical and mental one, as well. You need to spend a lot of time thinking about the music before it's ever played. And, don't ever think that conducting an orchestra isn't hard work. It is. They say that conductors live longer than anyone else because of the cardiovascular workout we get."

scholarship or grant money, the expense of the education and training necessary to become an orchestra conductor can be prohibitive.

Perks

For someone who loves music, there may be no better career than that of an orchestra conductor. Conducting assures that you'll spend time working with talented musicians, studying the works of great composers and bringing music to life for others who appreciate it.

Get a Jump on the Job

If you're not in an orchestra now, consider joining either your school orchestra or a community group. Most high school bands, orchestras, and choral groups sometimes allow students to perform as guest conductors for a particular piece. If you think this might be a career for you, see if your school's conductor will allow you to fledge your conducting wings.

Volunteer to play in pit orchestras for musical shows, both in your school and for community theater groups. If your town or city has a community orchestra, find out who conducts it and contact him or her. Attend musical performances, or even watch televised performances, and observe the conductor closely.

You might consider going to college to get a teaching degree first, so that you can teach music and gain experience by conducting a school musical group.

POSTPRODUCTION SUPERVISOR

OVERVIEW

You can't just film the ending credits of a movie or television show, package up the film reel, and send it merrily on its way to the theater or TV studio. A lot of work is necessary between the time the actual production ends and the time the film is ready to be released—editing, cuts, voice-overs, and much more. All those jobs are part of the *postproduction process*, and the many tasks involved are expected to be completed within an established budget and time frame.

As you might imagine, things can get a little tense at this stage of a film project. There are lots of different people involved in postproduction, all looking to see that their particular part of the project gets the money it needs to keep moving along. Many times, people don't agree on how the process should proceed or where the budgeted money should be spent. The entertainment industry is a lot about ego and getting your own way.

To keep the postproduction process moving and everyone working together somewhat harmoniously toward the goal, a postproduction supervisor rides herd on the entire crew. It's the job of the postproduction supervisor to coordinate the necessary processes and make sure the project moves ahead on schedule and stays on budget. He or she is accountable for overseeing everything from color grading to the hiring of video editors to film

AT A GLANCE

Salary Range

A postproduction supervisor can expect to earn between $1,500 and $3,000 a week. Postproduction supervisors recently were admitted as part of the Editor's Guild, which guarantees a pension, health care, and collective bargaining, in addition to the salary.

Education/Experience

There are no firm educational requirements for a postproduction supervisor, but most employers will look for a degree in theater arts or another related program. Because postproduction involves a wide range of disciplines, a liberal arts degree providing a wide scope also might be beneficial. Some employers require only a high school degree, but would expect extensive technical training and experience.

Personal Attributes

You should have good organizational skills and be an excellent communicator because you'll need to work with many different people in various roles. You should be detail oriented, assertive enough to keep production moving along, and able to work as part of a team. Because you'll inevitably be dealing with difficult situations, it's necessary to be able to think on your feet and make quick decisions in the midst of chaos. Being able to solve problems, soothe egos, and bring people and ideas together are important.

Requirements

A thorough understanding of the postproduction process and the ability to juggle more than one project at a time. You will need to have knowledge of all areas of production, and a substantial amount of hands-on experience in various jobs. Some employers may require union membership.

(continues)

AT A GLANCE *(continued)*

Outlook

Jobs in the entertainment industry, including those for postproduction supervisors, are expected to increase by between 10 and 20 percent through the year 2012. That job growth is considered to be average, according to government statistics.

voice-overs. In short, the postproduction supervisor is responsible for the creative and business aspects of the postproduction process.

He or she may hire editors or approve editors that someone else hires, and then attend editing sessions and confer with editors regularly about their progress. The postproduction supervisor chooses or approves postproduction facilities such as labs and reviews the dailies, which are the portions of film that come back from the developer on a daily basis. The supervisor schedules postproduction jobs such as final cuts and air dates, supervises music and sound effects, maintains quality control, and coordinates all technical needs.

People in this position normally have years of experience in the entertainment industry and have a thorough understanding of all the areas they oversee. In addition to technical experience, a postproduction supervisor must be mature and savvy enough to handle potentially explosive situations and to work as a mediator between creative people in different areas.

Most postproduction people have worked their way up from jobs such as a producer's assistant, apprentice, assistant editor, or postproduction assistant. A good attitude and level of enthusiasm will go a long way toward your advancement from one job to another.

Once they reach the level of postproduction supervisor, most people work on a freelance basis, although some television and film studios have postproduction supervisors on staff. Working as a freelance postproduction supervisor means that you need to get your name out on industry directories and know where to look for work.

Pitfalls

As with nearly all jobs in the entertainment industry, postproduction supervisor spots are competitive. You'll probably need to have quite a bit of experience under your belt before you'll be considered for this position, and, once you've got your foot in the door, there could be some lapses between jobs until you've established a sound reputation within the industry.

Once you get there, you'll have to deal with a very demanding job that can be stressful because you're expected to make sometimes-impossible deadlines while juggling different political factions who may not all see things in the same way.

Perks

Postproduction supervisors generally are highly regarded and respected within the entertainment industry. You normally can command a good wage because your experience and ability are recognized. Because you're responsible for such a wide variety of processes and oversee people in

Mitchell Buroker, former postproduction supervisor

Mitchell Buroker got his start in the entertainment industry in the editing business, paying his dues as he worked his way up through the ranks. He eventually ended up working for Roger Corman, a screenwriter, producer, director, and distributor of more than 300 small, low-budget films. Buroker worked in different capacities on more than 40 films for Corman, but often assumed the job and responsibilities of postproduction supervisor. That, he says, increased his learning curve tremendously.

"That's what happens," Buroker says. "You just get thrown into a job and you figure it out." Figuring out the job of a postproduction supervisor, however, requires a lot of background knowledge and experience.

"It isn't a job you want to get into without having had adequate experience," Buroker says. "That's really inviting a train wreck."

Buroker was hired by HBO Original Films as a postproduction supervisor, where he further honed his skills.

To be effective as a postproduction supervisor, Buroker says, you need to be able to juggle tasks, interact with many different people, keep track of schedules, manage the business side of a production, and try to keep everyone happy while you're doing it. The job involves a lot of negotiating and re-negotiating, organizing schedules and projects, and keeping on top of everything going on.

"It's a lot of organizational work and balancing a lot of different things," Buroker says. "You don't necessarily have the final word on everything, but it's an important position. What you are is the middle person. You're the voice of reason. The voice of calm."

The job of a postproduction supervisor is increasingly difficult, Buroker says, because you're given less and less time to do all the necessary work. If there is a delay somewhere during the preproduction or production periods, postproduction is sure to feel the pressure to make up the time and remain on schedule. "There's always a lot of rushing and pressure to get things done," Buroker says. "That pressure detracts from the ability to take your time with what you're trying to accomplish."

Still, he thinks working as a postproduction supervisor is fun because it entails so many different areas of the process. The job requires a range of experience within the film industry and a broad and thorough understanding of all that is involved. In addition, you should possess a level of maturity and be able to handle yourself well in a variety of situations.

While a college degree is important for someone who wants to be a postproduction supervisor, it's not absolutely necessary, and it shouldn't necessarily be film or entertainment related. His own degree from St. John's College in Annapolis, Maryland, is in philosophy, which he explained provided a range of knowledge and a broad view. In his opinion, Buroker says, film schools are overrated.

"Everyone who gets out of film school has to go back and start at the bottom of the pile," he says. "As long as you're bright and enthusiastic, nobody really cares if you went to film school or not. I think a college degree is important, but I don't think it [your major] has to be in film."

many different jobs, it's a safe bet that your work will not be repetitive or boring.

Get a Jump on the Job
Start learning what you can about film and television work in whatever way possible. Read books, make your own movies, and talk to anyone you know who has expertise in your area of interest. Some communities offer film classes or even filmmaking camps for young people. Keep your eyes and ears open to find out what's available, or use the Internet to find opportunities in your area.

PRODUCT PLACEMENT SPECIALIST

OVERVIEW

You're sitting in a darkened theater, eating popcorn and drinking soda, when suddenly you notice that your favorite actor is drinking the same brand of cola in the movie you're watching. Coincidence? Hardly.

It's all a part of product placement (or "entertainment marketing," as the industry prefers)—the efforts of companies to get their products featured prominently in a movie. An important placement can mean a windfall for the company. For example, Hershey experienced a popularity upsurge when everybody's favorite alien, E.T., gobbled up Reese's Pieces in front of captivated young audiences around the world. Soon every kid on the block was pestering Mom to buy the favored snack food of the wizened little space traveler.

Of course, E.T. wasn't the first star to use a popular product. Giveaways have been going on since the 1930s and 1940s, when actors were asked to boost certain products by using them. At that time, product placement was more a matter of convincing the star to use your item—such as getting Humphrey Bogart to sport the latest Gruen timepiece, a gift from the watch manufacturer.

Once mainly found only on the big screen, today product placement has been making quite a few appearances on TV—not to mention in video games and even books. Of course, a certain amount of discretion

AT A GLANCE

Salary Range
$30,000 to $120,000+, plus bonuses and commissions.

Education/Experience
Degree in marketing, advertising, or business.

Personal Attributes
Outgoing personality, ability to multi-task, ability to handle deadlines.

Requirements
None.

Outlook
This is a growing industry with great potential for newcomers.

is required when "planting" products in a film—you can go overboard and be too obvious with brand-name items as props within the context of a movie, television show, or music video. Clever marketing people aim to have their products visible but not the focus of the action. When done correctly, product placement adds a sense of realism to a movie or TV show. Watching a hero reach for a can of Dr. Pepper, for example, feels more real than if he grabbed a can with a generic "soda" label.

Of course, the effectiveness of this kind of advertising is hard to measure, but it's a lot cheaper than buying a 60-second spot on prime-time TV.

Sometimes product placement just happens. A set dresser, the producer, the director, or an actor might decide that a certain product will enhance the film, and it will simply be inserted into the movie. In this case, the manufacturer is never asked. In making the character's life seem real, products necessarily come into play.

However, most product placements are arranged—either placement in exchange for a supply of product, or placement because the film company is paid to include the product. Most often, it's a simple exchange. If a movie calls for a young, attractive surfer to gulp down a beverage, and someone on the crew knows the product placement specialist who handles Coke, the movie people approach the Coke product placement specialist, and they make a deal. In exchange for the airtime, the cast and crew are provided with a limitless supply of various Coke beverages during shooting. The production company saves money in beverage bills, Coke gets a free placement, the product placement specialist earns her commission, and everyone is happy.

Linda Swick, president and owner, product placement company

She prefers to call it "entertainment marketing" or "brand integration," but product placement is pretty much what Linda Swick has been doing for the past 18 years—and loving it. "I love the diversity of this job," she says. "Every day, I'm doing something different."

She started out working for a producer, and she was working for a casting director when she heard the editor of *Hollywood Reporter* speak. "He was saying that the 60-second commercial will someday go away, and that product placement was going to be very important to advertisers."

That made sense to Swick, who leaped on a subsequent opportunity to join a product placement corporation. "Back then, no one knew what it was," she laughs. After that company closed, she started her own company, International Promotions, where she's been happily handling products ever since.

Her clients include Ben and Jerry's, Dippin' Dots, Snap-on Tools, and Heinz ketchup, and it's her job to make sure these products show up on the big screen. "Sometimes clients hear about us from another company, and they'll come to us," she says. At other times, she'll read a script in which the young star is eating peanut butter, and she'll realize there's an opportunity to place a peanut butter company.

"We have major contacts with all the studios," she explains, "and they send us their scripts." Most of the time, the company does not pay to have its products featured in a film. "Instead, they'll donate props. For example, we'll outfit a film with a Dippin' Dots cart, get it to the set for them, do the coordination. It saves the director a lot of trouble." And the return, of course, is basically a free advertisement for whatever product is prominently displayed in the movie.

"We try to create placement for our products, but it's always a different script, a different scenario," she says. "It might be a TV show, a feature film, a reality show, and there are all different kinds of personalities, directors, prop masters, producers, wardrobe people, transportation coordinators. It's very exciting if you like to juggle multiple projects at one time. If you can't multi-task, this isn't the job for you!"

A typical day in a product placement specialist's life sounds like something out of a movie star magazine—attend a film screening, meet an actor over lunch, check with an agent, go out for a Hollywood gala in the evening. Lots of business gets done by referrals, and referrals happen over lunch and at parties and get-togethers. The product placement specialist is the one who reads the scripts, notes where a product might be placed, and contacts the director.

Pitfalls

As exciting as this job can be, it's also filled with stress, pressure, and sometimes impossible deadlines. You've got to be able to schmooze while juggling 10 different tasks at once.

Perks

If you're successful, the money—along with the commissions and bonuses—can be terrific. And for those who are movie-mad, living and working in Hollywood can be heady stuff. You'll be hobnobbing with directors, producers, and actors themselves in a job that's always different and plenty exciting.

Get a Jump on the Job

In college you'll want to concentrate on marketing, public relations, and business courses. If you live near California, where most of the product placement firms are located, you can try to wrangle a summer job or internship.

PROP MASTER

OVERVIEW

Whether a script calls for Colonial-style wooden buttons, an antique dentist's chair, or a 1950s-era silver toaster, the job of ferreting out the exact item falls to the prop master (short for *property master*). But whether you end up schlepping furniture around the set or painting scenery, it all depends on where you work and how the prop master job is described. That's why most good prop masters are jacks-of-all-trades. As a prop master, resourcefulness will serve you well.

Technically, a prop master is responsible for supplying and supervising all the props necessary for a production. Props may be defined differently from production to production, according to the availability of other crew members. If there's a set decorator, for instance, he or she might take care of getting furniture and other items that appear on the set, leaving the prop master to supply only the items that the actors and actresses hold in their hands.

Once a property budget has been established, the prop master works within that budget to find and maintain everything necessary for the performance. Inventiveness and ingenuity come in handy when the necessary items can't be located and have to be manufactured or tracked down by any means available.

You might think it would be easy to round up necessary props—but that's not always so. One online discussion board for prop people (PropPeople.com Discussion Board) is filled with frantic messages from props people looking for things like matching baby carriages from the 1950s, witch staffs, a fake 1943 Army issue .45 pistol, cheap "I Like Ike" campaign buttons, and an inflatable banana.

AT A GLANCE

Salary Range

There's a very wide salary range for prop masters, depending on the type of production, location, whether the person has union credentials, if the job is permanent or temporary, and other factors. A full-time prop master working for a major studio can earn more than $100,000 a year, while a prop master for a summer theater group might earn $250 a week, plus housing.

Education/Experience

There are no set educational requirements to work as a prop master, but most employers prefer a degree in theater arts or a related area.

Personal Attributes

You should be a problem solver and able to deal with sometimes difficult situations quickly and decidedly. You also need good communication skills in order to work with other crew members to determine just what sort of props are necessary to the production. You should be a team player and not be afraid to ask people (even people you don't know) for help.

Requirements

Some employers require membership in an industry union. You may need to have a car or van in which to transport props and a valid driver's license. You also will need to be willing to travel and be mechanically gifted.

Outlook

Jobs as a prop master are expected to increase by between 10 and 20 percent through the year 2012, according to government statistics. That job growth is considered to be average.

Other sources for obtaining property are period stores, property houses, specialty property houses, and promotional property houses. Property houses offer a wide variety of items that might be necessary for a production—including caskets, artificial rocks, live trees, sleighs, Little League baseball equipment, Christmas decorations, indoor furniture, and park benches. Specialty property houses might concentrate on only one type of prop, such as firearms, or they might build props to meet the specifications of clients.

Promotional property houses (also called product placement agencies) work for businesses or companies to promote their products or services by having them appear on a television show or in a film or theater production. A car manufacturer, for instance, might be very anxious to have the glamorous star of a feature film driving a particular kind of car. Product placement agencies are happy to provide props at no cost in order to gain exposure for their clients.

Prop masters work in many different settings and capacities, hired by everybody from big-budget feature films to summer stock theater productions. Big-name productions typically have more money, so they can hire bigger crews with members who have more specialized skills. For

Cathy T. Marshall, prop master

When it comes to props, Cathy Marshall has done it all. President of the New York prop firm Marshall Arts, Inc., she's well known as a prop master and works regularly in both props and set design. She has worked on TV sets, decorated corporate offices, and provides and manages props for commercials. One thing she'll tell you for sure is that when she's working, no two days are the same.

"I might spend one day drawing set sketches and communicating with an agency or director about the direction they want to go as far as the set and the props go," Marshall says. "Another day I'll be running around prop houses in New York or New Jersey, looking for the right pieces, photographing them, and taking the photos to the director or agency so they can make the final picks."

Other days might be spent cataloging and preparing props for storage, while on shoot days her primary concern is to get everything on set and ready to shoot smoothly. "There's no time then for a forgotten or misplaced prop," Marshall says.

Marshall entered the world of props while she was still in college in Atlanta, working on a fine arts degree. A New York production company filming monthly commercials in Atlanta for a large retail store hired her to be a production assistant when its crew was working there. "Basically, I was a gofer they called a production assistant," Marshall recalls. Eventually, however, she moved into using props to create many different looks within the house where the commercials were shot. She discovered that she enjoyed the creative aspect of prop work, and except for a short time in production, she's been working in that field ever since.

"I got bored with producing and decided to set up a company to give me a creative outlet of designing sets and propping, which are the things I love to do. Now my life is never boring, and often it's incredibly fun!"

instance, a major production probably will hire an outdoor prop person to track down props, and an indoor prop person to work with the props in front of the camera. Smaller productions, however, usually only have one person handle both jobs, and are more likely to prefer crew members who are more versatile.

Prop masters may work with directors, costume designers, set decorators, set designers, production designers, producers, or special effects coordinators to determine exactly what types of props are necessary and what they should look like. It may be necessary to gather hundreds of items as props. Determining what props are neces-sary also requires a thorough knowledge of the script.

Pitfalls

While you may be able to find prop master positions available for summer theater groups and small, local shows, the competition for jobs on top television and film productions is keen. Usually, only very experienced people are hired for major productions, which means you'll probably have to start out in relatively low paying jobs. You also may be required to obtain union membership before landing a job, which can be difficult. However, working

During her years as a prop master, Marshall has been charged with locating some pretty unusual items, including a Chinese rickshaw, a 1957 Chevy, a 1961 pink Cadillac, a llama, a London phone booth, and a set of fire hydrants. "I sometimes feel like I'm on a scavenger hunt for unusual or unique things," Marshall says. "It's important to have sources where you know you'll find as many things as possible. Someone e-mailed me recently looking for a source to find a stuffed alligator for a student film. I was able to tell him three different places to look."

Resourcefulness and the ability to solve problems is no less important once the sets have been acquired, Marshall says. Often, she'll need to make a rig or to wire an object in exactly the right spot on a set. Because much of her work is for commercials, Marshall finds herself working in various locations, including private homes. Working in someone's home puts additional pressure on her as a prop person.

"I'm always mindful of being in someone's home," she says, "and have to be very careful that none of the props we're using cause any damage to the home. If they do, it's my job to repair any scratches or clean up a mess."

In addition to being naturally creative and a good problem solver, Marshall attributes her success to the fact that she's versatile and able to work in many capacities on a set. She moves heavy furniture, knows what type of spray will make a toaster less shiny, hangs and rigs props, and unwraps and rewraps them for shipping.

"Every job is different and has a whole new list of needs," Marshall says. "A prop person should be mechanically gifted and know what tool works best for what job. I've had to create a steam rig to make a big pot of steaming pasta for a Ragu commercial. You never know. It's always different."

for small companies will help you in getting a union card and increase your chances of landing a job with a major house.

Perks

If you are creative, love to be challenged, and enjoy being around other creative people, the job of a prop master is probably a good fit. If you love to shop, you'll have plenty of opportunity, and there is great satisfaction in searching for and finding a one-of-a-kind item that is absolutely necessary to the production.

Get a Jump on the Job

Get involved in theater productions in your school, place of worship, or community and offer to work on obtaining and managing props. Learn all that you can about period clothing, furniture, and styles in order to get a sense of the type of props that would be appropriate in different settings. Talk to anyone you know who works in theater or with film or television and ask for advice and contacts. Develop your artistic skills, get some kind of art or theater education, expect to start in a ground-level position, and be patient.

PUPPETEER

OVERVIEW

Long before Oscar the Grouch first popped out of his trash can, or Punch first whacked Judy on the streets of London, puppets and puppeteers have been plying their trade, delighting audiences everywhere. Puppets have been discovered in the great pyramids of Egypt, and references are made to puppets in writings from ancient Greece and the Roman Empire. They were used in churches during the Middle Ages, but later became more common as entertainment at street fairs, carnivals, and parties. Puppets were popular during Renaissance times, when puppeteers entertained everyone from kids to kings.

While puppet shows are typically assumed to appeal to children, puppets also have been used in opera and serious theater productions. Puppets have enjoyed renewed popularity over the past decades as TV characters, such as the famous muppets of the TV show *Sesame Street*.

Without puppeteers, however, puppets are just lifeless pieces of wood and styrofoam. It is the puppeteer who creates the puppet show, who makes and costumes the puppets, and gives them movement and voice. It is the puppeteer who brings the puppet to life. They may write original scripts for their puppets to perform, build puppet theaters, sew clothing for their puppets, talk and sing for their puppets, and animate them either manually or mechanically.

Different types of puppets are operated in different ways. Marionettes are operated by strings, while rod puppets are moved

AT A GLANCE

Salary Range

A full-time puppeteer working for a small entertainment business can expect to earn between $15,000 and $20,000 a year to start. A professional puppeteer who designs, builds, and performs with puppets on Broadway, on the other hand, may make well over $100,000 a year. How much money you can expect to make as a puppeteer depends on many factors, including your level of experience, how well known you are as a puppeteer, and the type of puppetry you perform.

Education/Experience

There are no established educational requirements for puppeteers. A degree in theater arts would provide a good background for working in puppetry. There are very few colleges in the United States that offer degrees in puppetry, although a variety of colleges and universities offer puppetry courses.

Personal Attributes

Should be determined and willing to work very hard in order to succeed; must be physically fit and agile (puppetry involves a lot of crawling around and getting into weird positions), and, depending on the type of puppetry, able to work for long periods of time without stopping. Creativity is essential, as puppeteers tend to work in many areas of puppetry. A good sense of humor is highly desirable.

Requirements

Requirements vary, depending on the type of puppetry work you get involved with. Television and film puppeteers, for instance, need to have some mechanical ability because they use animatronic controllers and other sophisticated equipment. Marionette puppeteers need to have excellent hand-eye coordination. People who work with bigger-than-life-sized puppets must have training in theatrical movement and positioning.

(continues)

AT A GLANCE (continued)

Outlook

Jobs in the field of puppetry are expected to increase by between 10 and 20 percent through the year 2012. That job growth is considered to be average. Keep in mind, however, that some areas of puppetry—especially TV and film puppetry—are more competitive than other areas.

by a rod that extends the amount of space between the puppet and the puppeteer. A puppeteer using hand puppets uses hands, fingers, and wrists to animate the characters. Movie and TV puppets might move via remote control.

The type of training you'll need depends largely on what type of puppetry you plan to perform. It's important, however, not to limit yourself to just one area of puppetry. You'll have a much better chance of finding work if you're somewhat versatile. It also helps if you can perform multiple functions of puppetry, such as designing and building your own puppets, writing your own scripts, and performing various voices for different puppet characters.

While there are many puppeteers, there are very few who manage to make a living being one. Most puppeteers work at other jobs in addition to puppetry work. If you dream of working as a puppeteer, you may be hired to perform in schools, at parties and other special events, or in libraries, theaters, and other locales.

Puppets remain popular at fairs and carnivals, but also are used to re-enact classic theater and opera. The area of puppetry is as wide open as your imagination, but you'll need to be willing to

work hard to prepare a show that sets you apart from other puppeteers. If you're very lucky, you might get a job assisting an established puppeteer, which may provide both income and invaluable training experience.

Pitfalls

Many puppeteers find it difficult to make a living in puppetry work and find they must hold other jobs in order to supplement their incomes. You might experience lapses in employment as a puppeteer, as the work tends to be irregular. Work as a puppeteer can be both physically and mentally demanding, as it can require extensive movement and the need for complete concentration.

Perks

If you love puppets, what could be more fun than being a puppeteer? Puppetry is a great way to relate messages. If you have a particular area of interest, such as conflict resolution or promoting respect among groups, you can use your puppets to communicate the message. People who work in puppetry tend to be fun and outgoing types who enjoy camaraderie and association with other puppeteers. In other words, you'll be in good company.

Get a Jump on the Job

Nearly everyone gets into puppetry differently. You can get a head start by either buying some puppets or making your own, and then practicing like crazy. If you can't find a puppetry organization in your area, there are online puppet groups that will enable you to be in contact with other puppet enthusiasts and share concerns, questions, and ideas. There also are books on puppetry that can help you get started. (See the books listed in *Read More About It* at the back of this book.) Once you've gained some experience, you can check out summer puppetry festivals held in various locations across the country. These give you the opportunity to perform, as well as offer workshops and training.

Rick Lyon, professional puppeteer

Rick Lyon estimates that he's one of only a few dozen people in the United States who make their living as a professional puppeteer. He modestly attributes his achievement to a great love of puppetry and a great deal of discipline, but stops short of calling himself successful.

"Well, success is for someone else to judge, I think," Lyon says. "But I manage to make a living doing what I do by dedicating myself wholeheartedly to it. By being excited enough by what I do to do it all the time. Like listening to a favorite record or watching a favorite movie over and over, it's something I never get tired of because I love puppetry."

His love of puppetry, however, is not all it takes to be a full-time, professional puppeteer. "Making a living in the arts is hard," Lyon says. "It takes more than just the love of something—you also have to develop great discipline. You have to practice and keep learning to be better at what you do."

Lyon's impressive resume (you can check it out on his Web site at http://www.lyonpuppets. com) includes feature films, TV shows, music videos, educational videos, commercials and industrial work. He creates and makes puppets, writes scripts and music for his own shows, directs puppet action, and even built and performed for the puppets in *Avenue Q*, a Broadway show that won a Tony Award for Best Musical in 2004. He's worked for the late Jim Henson (founder of *Sesame Street*), Columbia Pictures, ABC, CBS, PBS, the Disney Channel, Comedy Central, Fox TV, Nickelodeon, and VH1.

When he's not puppeteering for television or films, Lyon performs with his own troupe, The Lyon Puppets, for which he makes the puppets and writes the scripts and music. "I get to exercise every creative muscle I have," Lyon says. "I design my puppets, which means deciding on how they'll look. I make my puppets, which means deciding how they'll work. And, I perform my puppets, which means deciding how they will act. I also write scripts and music for my own shows. So, I get to do a little bit of everything."

Lyon's educational background includes studying theater arts at Penn State University and puppetry at the Institute of Professional Puppetry Arts in Connecticut. He also studied at the Institut Internationale de la Marionnette in France. His fascination with puppets, however, began very early in his life.

"I don't remember a time when I wasn't interested in puppetry," Lyon says. "It has always been a part of my life. At first it was a hobby—something to do just for fun. When I was a kid, I used to do puppet shows for my family and friends in my basement. Eventually, I started doing performances in school and church. At first I used store-bought puppets, but very quickly started making my own. By the time I was 10 years old I was making all my own puppets."

(continues)

(continued)

Lyon's schedule is hectic, to say the least. While performing with *Avenue Q*, as he was at the time this was written, a typical day might be working with his staff in his workshop during the morning, designing and building puppets to be used either in his own shows or for other purposes. In the afternoon he might take a few hours to work on the business side of his business, ordering supplies, paying bills, and scheduling appointments. Those, Lyon says, are his least favorite aspects of being a professional puppeteer. "I'd rather be creative all day, but sometimes you have to stop and take care of business," he says.

At the end of the work day, he goes home to eat a quick dinner, shower, shave, and take a bus from his home outside of the city into New York to perform on Broadway. "My normal working day is very long," Lyon says. "I work in my workshop all day, then perform on Broadway until late at night."

Still, Lyon wouldn't have it any other way. His work has put him in contact with TV personalities, rock stars, actors and actresses, and a lot of great puppets. He's worked with everyone from business executives to singer David Bowie to *Sesame Street's* Bert, Ernie, Oscar the Grouch, Big Bird, and Cookie Monster. He marvels every day at how fortunate he is to be able to have so much fun at a job that he loves.

If you're interested in puppetry, Lyon recommends that you watch as much puppetry as you can, in live shows, TV, films, or video. Watch the movements of the puppets carefully, he says, and take note of what you like and don't like. Learn all you can about puppetry by reading books and articles and talking to puppeteers—and practice. "Practice until your arms fall off," Lyon says. "Videotape your practice sessions then look back at them with a critical eye as to how you can improve. Then practice some more."

Once you've got a show, get out there and perform it for whoever will watch, Lyon says. Volunteer to be the entertainment at birthday parties, your church or synagogue, and at school events. Because there is not a lot of formal training available for puppeteers, you'll need to be creative and persistent in your learning.

"You basically have to learn from other people who are already puppeteers, and teach yourself," Lyon says, noting that you can study puppetry in college. "The University of Connecticut is a school with one of the best puppetry programs," he says. "There are some summer puppetry festivals that have workshops. Mostly, though, it's just watching and learning and practicing and working some more."

SCENE CONSTRUCTION EXPERT

OVERVIEW

If you like the idea of reproducing a woman's hands in detail 20 feet high, making giant inflatable rocks, or building a two-story house to fit on a Broadway stage, scene construction could be the career for you. These experts make sets for stage, video, and TV productions, and run their own set construction workshops, interpreting the production and designing the physical elements of both stage and settings. Scene construction experts also collaborate with the director and other designers to make a production look just right. The setting of a show helps to visually explain to the audience what's happening, so how it looks is vitally important.

As a scene construction worker, you'll work primarily as a freelancer, although some theaters, TV companies, and scenic workshops may hire full-time set construction experts.

Although studios and other production companies are responsible for financing, producing, publicizing, and distributing a film or program, scene construction experts (or master carpenters, as they're also known) are often the most valuable people in the theater, because they know what's safe and what isn't, and what staging will and won't work. The actual making of a production is completed by hundreds of independent contractors hired on an as-needed basis who build the very sets you see on TV and in the movies.

AT A GLANCE

Salary Range
$200 to $400 a day.

Education/Experience
A course in scenic design will teach you techniques such as marbling, ragging, and wood-graining, as well as how to organize your materials, your budget, and your time, but construction experience is the most important thing. Anyone interested in pursuing a career in theater construction or carpentry work to gain a background in engineering or trades.

Personal Attributes
Flexibility, ability to get along with others, a cool head, ability to deal with stressful situations.

Requirements
Building skill, attention to detail, ability to meet deadlines.

Outlook
Excellent. There are always talented construction crews needed to build sets in California, and anywhere else movie-making goes on.

For example, in the movie *Christmas with the Kranks*, producers needed to come up with a very specific street that was described in great detail in the script—particularly the way the different neighbors' homes connected. The street needed its own personality with houses that were alike in design but different in character. Since the filmmakers were never able to find exactly what they needed in real life, they decided to build an entire town—complete with snow—on a parking lot in the former Boeing aircraft factory in Downey, California, about 15 miles from downtown Los Angeles. Each and every one of the 16 houses on the set was carefully constructed, built to local codes, in three months from start to the first day of shooting. It was a huge task involving crowds of carpenters, plasterers, electricians, and painters building what turned out to be one of the largest exterior sets ever built for a movie—more than 700 feet from one end to the other. The sidewalks and driveways were designed to reveal years of wear and tear. Soil and full-grown trees were trucked in, lawns were planted, and snow was sifted over everything. In fact, this is one of the most important things in set construction—the work must be to the highest standard, cost effective, and still come in within budget.

Once the designers come up with a look, the scene construction crew come in and build the set according to the plans they've been given, either on location or on a soundstage.

The methods used to construct a set—which nowadays can include using steel or aluminum, not just wood—is

Tim Harriss, scene construction expert

Most scene workers are hired to complete tasks ranging from basic house painting to preparing faux finishings, backdrops, and murals, as well as aging items, such as making a wagon wheel that looks old. For Tim Harriss, it seemed like an interesting way to make a living.

A musician and artist, Harriss got into the business via a friend, who was busy with set construction work and couldn't handle all the work. "I decided to try it out," Harriss says. With a solid background in art, he was soon able to parlay his skill into his own set construction jobs. Since that first job, he's constructed sets for a series of B movies, the *Hannibal* set, and lots of commercials for the Virginia lottery.

"The film business... it's just a very nuts way to make a living," Harriss says. "You lose your life. When a production is going on, you're working 12 hours a day, six days a week. You have to be flexible. Sometimes you have to work far away."

When it comes to location work, Harriss says he prefers building in the shop doing preproduction work. "We went in on a soundstage, built sets and painted them, and then the set dressers would bring in the decorations, and then the lighting people would come in. We were several steps ahead of the actual production crew on the set, and that was kind of nice."

Production on a major film or production can be incredibly intense. "It's a super hectic environment to be in," Harriss says. "I prefer to be away from that. There are a lot of egos." However, some set construction experts must be present on set during filming, ready to fix something that breaks or repair an item.

"The money is really good, but there's a trade-off—you lose your ability to do anything else, and the burnout rate is pretty high, too," he says. On the other hand, there is a lot of work available if you're handy with a hammer, and there always seems to be filming going on—and not just in Los Angeles. "There's a lot of work in Maryland, in Baltimore, and in Wilmington, North Carolina," Harriss says. "It's crazy, interesting work and you meet a lot of interesting people."

decided by safety, cost, and the practical operation of the set. In addition, if the set is touring it must be constructed in a way that it breaks into manageable sections to accommodate the various theaters. Once the basic construction is complete, the scene construction experts move on to the next job, leaving the next steps for the set dressers and designers, who place the finishing decorations on the set, followed by the electricians and lighting crews.

Building sets isn't usually a leisurely affair. By the time the designers have created the right look that they want, there isn't usually lots of time to spend leisurely constructing. Instead, the construction site tends to be an intense, hectic few weeks, with long days and six- or seven-day weeks. When it's over, the expert moves on to the next job.

Pitfalls

Because most of these jobs are union, it can be tough to get a start. Joining a union can be a frustrating task, as candidates must fulfill a wide range of requirements.

Perks

If you're a skilled construction worker, it can be fun (and lucrative) to work in film construction. As a freelancer, you'll also have independence and a certain amount of autonomy.

Get a Jump on the Job

You don't have to wait until you're in college to start building sets. Practical construction experience is invaluable, so you could start by volunteering with your local theater or school drama group. Your art class also may help prepare sets for a school play, so check out these possibilities. Theater clubs also can provide experience. In addition, you may want to check out various courses available in art, painting, construction techniques, welding, and computers that would be helpful.

SCREENWRITER

OVERVIEW

Back in the days of the silent pictures, you didn't need a brilliant screenwriter to have a hit on your hands. But once the talkies were invented, film studios realized they'd need to hire some top talent to write fabulous lines for their actors to speak. Some of the country's best writers, including William Faulkner and F. Scott Fitzgerald, soon found themselves earning up to $1,500 a week by turning out screenplays, at a time when the average worker's weekly salary was just $10.

People have been romanticizing the life of a screenwriter ever since, imagining a glamorous career spent sitting around in casual outfits, drinking coffee, pounding out scripts, earning big money, and hanging around with a Hollywood crowd. The reality is often far from this exciting picture.

It all begins with an idea that a screenwriter must turn into a script. This means that either the writer comes up with his or her own theme, or they transform an existing piece of writing and adapt it into a screenplay or television pilot (a sample episode of a proposed TV series). Screenwriters work closely with producers and directors.

Next, if you're a budding screenwriter and you have an original screenplay to be produced, first you have to find an agent to read it. Without an agent, no major studio will even look at your material. Studios rely on agents to filter through the thousands of junky screenplays to find what they consider to be quality material. Many new screenwriters try to get their work

AT A GLANCE

Salary Range

Feature-film screenwriters' pay is comparable to a director's or producer's salary, and can range to the high six figures.

Education/Experience

Although many screenwriters have college degrees, talent and creativity are even more important determinants of success in the industry. In addition to colleges and technical schools, many private institutes offer training programs on various aspects of filmmaking, such as screenwriting. For example, the American Film Institute offers training in screenwriting as well as directing, production, cinematography, and production design.

Personal Attributes

Self-motivation, perseverance, and an ability to take criticism.

Requirements

Screenwriters need to develop creative writing skills, a mastery of film language, and a basic understanding of filmmaking. Screenwriters must believe in what they're doing and in their ability, and be able to defend their ideas.

Outlook

Employment of screenwriters is expected to grow about as fast as the average for all occupations through the year 2012, according to the Bureau of Labor Statistics. The outlook is expected to be competitive, because many people with writing or journalism training are attracted to this job. Although there are more opportunities for women now in this business, it's widely acknowledged in Hollywood that the situation remains very difficult for women and screenwriters over age 30.

produced by an independent producer or student film producers, so they will have a

Susan Kouguell, screenwriter

It was in college that Susan Kouguell and a friend first started writing short films, all six of which ended up in the Metropolitan Museum of Art. Less than a year after ending her collaboration, she was hired to write her first feature.

Today, she's an award-winning screenwriter and filmmaker. She co-wrote *The Suicide Club*, wrote voice-over narrations for *Murder One* and *Dakota* , and has done 11 feature film rewrites for independent production companies. As chair of her motion picture consulting company Su-City Pictures East, she has worked with more than 1,000 writers and filmmakers, as well as a range of studios including Miramax, Warner Bros., and Fine Line Features. She's also working on prose, a novel, short stories, script doctoring, and libretti for major symphonies, in addition to teaching screenwriting at Tufts University, teaching business writing at SUNY Purchase, while also teaching classes for screenwriters online.

Kouguell has a very personal connection to the business: Her great-great aunt was the great German actress Therese Giehse. When she was 11, Kouguell saw her first movie starring her famous aunt. "It changed me," she says. "To see her on film about a family hiding during World War II, there was a very personal connection there. Something lit up inside of me." In her early 20s, she introduced herself to her idol, the internationally known director Louis Malle, because so many of his movies had starred her aunt. Soon the two were working together. She emphasizes that she had been prepared for this meeting by working hard in school years before.

"You have to do the work," she says. "Your next-door neighbor can be Steven Spielberg, but if you don't have the training, it won't happen. You've got to go to school—even if not for filmmaking, learning as much as you can. Otherwise, those opportunities aren't going to pan out."

Still, despite all the training and connections, life is very tough for women screenwriters in Hollywood. "Everyone I know who has made it in Hollywood is male," she says. "None of my female friends have broken in. It's a club, and they're always looking for the next hot young thing, the young talent." There just isn't recognition and support—not just for women, but for anyone older than 30. "You walk into a meeting with an agent and they see you're over 30 or 40, they think that you might not have your finger on the pulse of what's happening, you might not be the right person because you're over a certain age."

"Screenwriting is especially tough for women in the industry," she says. "It's very competitive, and you have to make a commitment to write, to do the best work that you can, to have to have passion for it." Susan notes that today's screenwriters are facing a very different world from when she first started in the business. "Now because of the Internet, the *Today Show*, world news—everybody is always talking about box office gross. Kids are much more aware of the industry, and how much money you can make."

Still, she thinks the chances of selling a script for a million dollars are few and far between. "You have to feel passionate about filmmaking," she says. "You shouldn't think about: 'Oh, I'm going to get rich doing it!' Because the chances of that are very small."

(continues)

sample to show to a prospective agent. You can find independent or student producers advertising in screenwriting newsletters, offering little or no up-front money for the screenplays, but providing a way to get your work produced.

Once you have an agent, he or she will submit your screenplay to film companies, where it will be read by the company "reader"—usually an intern or a young college grad who's paid to make a decision about a daily pile of scripts quickly

(continued)

She encourages young filmmakers who are passionate about writing and filmmaking to start small, volunteering at film conferences and film festivals. Your economic background shouldn't be the reason for preventing you from getting a foot in the door," she insists.

"Today technology makes it much easier," she says. "Kids can go out with a digital camera and make something cheap, which is wonderful. There are so many more outlets too, so many more film festivals, cable outlets, than when I first started out. It's just that independent filmmaking is well regarded. You may not make big bucks, but you can find a way to make a living."

When she first started doing short films, she realized that as a screenwriter, she could touch people and make them think. "You may not like the writing I'm doing, but it's opening up a dialogue," she says. When her first film about World War II was picked up by the Museum of Modern Art and then shown at the Pompidou Center in Paris, it changed her life. "For me to be there, talking to a French audience and having to defend my work, it was great!" she says. "Some people loved it and others were questioning everything I wrote, but I felt I had done my job and was conveying ideas that were important, about the war and politics." Whether her audience agreed with her, she says, didn't matter. "To be talking to a European audience about my work when I was just in my mid-20s was amazing."

Later on, seeking to broaden her market, she started Su-city Pictures. "I realized there weren't hundreds of script consultants doing what I was doing," she says. "Now there are thousands. I created a niche for myself." Once you've found that niche and you're writing for films, you'll also need to keep in mind that the process is a collaboration. Kouguell suggests you think of your screenplay as a blueprint for many other people to work from, editing and applying their own vision. "It presents an interesting challenge to find a way to work in a collaborative way that's positive for you," she says. "It can be very exciting, but you need to develop a really tough skin. If somebody doesn't like my idea, I have to be open to understanding why and hammer this out together rather than thinking 'I stink.'"

You have to be passionate about screenwriting, and you have to be tough. "If you're a writer and you're getting rejected and rejected, you can say at least 'I've gotten feedback.'" You must strive to do your best work, she says. "It's really about perseverance," she insists. "You have to be a bulldozer."

In the end, she believes scriptwriters write because they have to write. "I didn't go into it to make money, I did it because I had to do it. You have to find something that's right for who you are… you have to be true to your vision, who you are as an artist and as a person."

(usually within the first 10 pages). Either it grabs them, or it doesn't; if it doesn't, you get a rejection letter. If it does, the reader forwards the script higher up the company chain for others to consider.

Many TV writers are hired based on a *spec script*—a sample script of a series that's already being produced. If you want to produce a spec script, you'd create an episode as if you were already a staff writer. If the show's producers think you've managed to capture the characters and voice, you may be invited to interview for a position on the show's writing staff. Sometimes you'll be asked to prepare a *shooting script*, which has instructions about shots, camera angles, and lighting.

Once your script is accepted, your work is far from over. Often screenwriters are asked to make changes in the script to reflect the ideas of the director, the producer, or even the actors. This means that not only do you need to be creative—you've also got to work well under pressure, writing and rewriting version after version of a script with just about everybody looking over your shoulder. Since time is money in the entertainment business, your ability to crank out work quickly is important.

Many screenwriters have a degree in writing, journalism, or English, and begin their careers as copywriters in advertising agencies or as writers for educational film companies, government audiovisual departments, or corporate film divisions. These jobs offer good training and a weekly paycheck. As they build a reputation in their career, demand for their screenplays or teleplays increases, and their earnings grow. Some eventually move on to become directors or producers.

While most writers for feature films are freelancers, TV shows typically hire a stable of writers they use from week to week. Staffing season (March through June) is when the bulk of these writers get their jobs on TV shows. Mid-season shows, however, don't hire staff during a specific time, so you should work closely with your agent about upcoming opportunities throughout the year. And keep writing, because the more screenplays you've written, the greater chance one of them will be produced, and even more important, the better you will learn the craft.

Pitfalls

Writing for Hollywood is a business that can break your heart, because for every success story there are hundreds of screenwriters who will never get anyone important to read a single word of their work. Screenwriting in Hollywood—especially in television—is particularly tough for women and for anyone over age 30, most screenwriters agree. It can be tough to see how your words are altered and changed by others involved in the production.

Perks

If you're successful, screenwriting can be a writer's dream: big money, exciting lifestyle, lots of recognition. To a screenwriter, nothing beats seeing your work up on the big screen.

Get a Jump on the Job

There are many ways to get your foot in the door. Some start by becoming a script reader—someone who evaluates and writes synopses of scripts for a literary production company or a network. Others become a production assistant, a writer's assistant, or an assistant to a producer. Writer training programs are another way to get experience.

Although you don't need to have an agent to get a job as a screenwriter, it is a bit daunting to get a writing job without some type of established legal representation. The Writers Guild of America can help you with your agent search; they've created a full-service Web site that has a lot of information that will help you further your understanding of the many aspects of the industry.

SET DESIGNER

OVERVIEW

If you've ever watched a movie or play and felt like you had been transported to another place or time, you can thank the set designer. Set designers are responsible for theater, television, and movie production sets, as well as commercial sets. Their job is to create authentic, believable-looking backgrounds that enhance the performances of actors and transport the audience to wherever the production is set.

The scope of a set designer's job varies greatly, depending on the size and budget of the production. Most set designer jobs are with large-production theater companies or movie studios, so you should be willing to go to where the work is. It only makes sense that there will be more opportunity for set designers in California or New York City than in a midwestern farm town. And, if a movie is filmed on location, a set designer must be willing to travel to the filming site.

A set designer might be directly responsible for creating the look of the set, or might take direction from an art director. If the responsibility is on the set designer, he or she normally begins by making freehand sketches of how the sets should look. The set designer would then work with the director of production, the production manager, and writers to finalize set concepts. Scale models must be made, and, once the plans have been finalized,

AT A GLANCE

Salary Range

The median salary for a set designer in the United States is $37,250, according to the Bureau of Labor Statistics. However, the salary of a set designer can be affected dramatically by factors such as the size of the employer, the budget of the project, and employee credentials and experience.

Education/Experience

Many set designers attend art schools or colleges with specialized programs in design. As with most jobs in the entertainment industry, however, people come into this job through different doors. Some set designers have learned the job through experience or come from a related profession, such as that of an interior designer. Some type of postsecondary education, however, probably will be necessary for this job.

Personal Attributes

Must be creative and artistic, and able to visualize what a set should look like, based on drawings or even verbal descriptions. You should have a good sense of how to convey emotion through surroundings, and how to create a mood. You also need a knack for arranging and decorating.

Requirements

With the proper education you might be able to land a job as a set designer without working your way up through the ranks of a production crew. However, you might have to pay your industry dues by working as a design assistant or production assistant. Some employers will require membership in an entertainment industry union.

Outlook

Jobs as set designer are expected to increase by between 10 and 20 percent through the year 2012. That job growth is considered to be average.

the set designer works with construction workers who actually build the sets.

A set designer is responsible for creating a mood and feeling for the production. The set must be believable, so that actors and actresses look at home on it. For instance, if the production features a single mother working two jobs and raising three young children, a set on which a living room is perfectly clean and arranged, with no clutter or signs of wear, would not be believable. The set designer is responsible for creating a background that looks like it belongs to three young children and a frazzled mom. Working with prop masters and set decorators, set designers also help to decide what items should appear on the set, including furniture, plants, drapes, and accessories.

Set design involves many skills, ranging from painting to choosing carpets to carpentry. If you're a set designer, you can expect to work long hours, and experience a significant amount of pressure. You'll need to be able to work within the production's budget, work closely with other production people, and communicate your ideas effectively.

Pitfalls

It will be difficult to find a job as a set designer without prior experience. You

---

Carol Cartwright, set designer

Carol Cartwright looks at every set design as a chance to express the personality of the actors and actresses involved. "We have to be sort of like psychologists," she says. "We need to think about how our characters are going to be different, and how the set will need to look in order for them to be able to do what they need to do. The set has to reflect the personality of the actor or actress, even when they're not there."

Cartwright, who has an undergraduate degree in sculpture, landed in set design after graduating from film school. While she originally intended to be a director, she soon realized that her interests remained with art. "The long and short of it is, I went to film school and decided I was more interested in directing art than in directing actors," she says.

She started working as an art director on low budget films and music videos, taking whatever jobs she could find until she was able to join the International Alliance of Theatrical and Stage Employees Union. "I sort of crawled up the ladder until I could get into the union," she says.

Finding jobs got easier after that, and Cartwright has been involved with a number of feature films and music videos, including Spike Lee's basketball film *He Got Game* and a biographical film about the late American abstract expressionist artist Jackson Pollack. Cartwright recommends that anyone interested in becoming a set designer get a strong art and/or theater background. And, she says, it's good to have a lot of energy, a willingness to work long days, and a good sense of humor.

"It's a kooky, nutty kind of job," Cartwright says. "It tends to have some strange parameters. Once you're in the union you can earn good money, but you have to sort of be on call. When you're working on a job, your phone will ring after you get home. And, if you're in your pajamas, you will put your clothing back on and go do what you need to do."

may need to be creative as you work to build a portfolio. And the work can involve long hours and a lot of stress, especially if the production has a quick-release date.

Perks

Theater and television people tend to be creative types with lots of energy and interests, making for an upbeat work environment. If you work on large productions with big-name performers, you might get to mingle with movie stars.

Get a Jump on the Job

Some level of set design is necessary for every production, from a little play in your basement, to a church production, to a school musical, to Broadway. Sign up to help with your high school productions, or look for a community theater group that will allow you to help with set design and construction. Computer-generated set design is becoming increasingly important, so if you enjoy computer graphics, you can work to develop your skills.

SET MEDIC

OVERVIEW

The actors are assembled, the clapper loader is poised, the director is ready to start the action, when suddenly a cry goes up—one of the child actors just got a splinter! *"Where's the medic? Get the medic!"*

Everything grinds to a halt as the set medic appears, Band-Aid and salve to the rescue. Just another patient in the medic's busy day on the set.

Whenever a cast and crew assembles to film a commercial, film, or TV show, a set medic is almost always required to be on hand to provide for the medical needs of the entire cast and crew. The medic is also the safety liaison between the production and construction crews, and various government agencies responsible for on-the-job safety. Set medics also are responsible for handling all the workers' comp paperwork, handling all the work-related injuries, and dealing with documentation on unsafe working conditions.

That may sound like quite a lot—but days may go by and the set medic gets nothing more serious to attend to than a headache or a case of hives. But you never know when the next emergency may occur. Should an elderly actor suddenly double over with a heart attack, the set medic's presence can spell the difference between life or death.

Surprisingly, a set medic doesn't have to be an EMT—a wide range of medical personnel can work on a set besides EMTs, including paramedics, nurses, and physicians—but regardless of the credentials, the pay and the job responsibilities are the same. Typically,

AT A GLANCE

Salary Range

Union scale is $27.25 an hour, with time and a half for overtime and double pay past 12 hours. Feature films may pay more, and commercials may pay up to $500 a day. May earn well over $100,000 a year.

Education/Experience

Medical personnel with varying levels of education can serve as set medics—from emergency medical technicians and paramedics to nurses and doctors.

Personal Attributes

Pleasant, friendly, and courteous. Should be flexible and willing to travel.

Requirements

Minimum medical certification as emergency medical technician basic, paramedic, registered nurse (RN), licensed practical nurse (LPN), or physician (MD).

Outlook

Good.

the set medic is on set from the beginning of preproduction or construction through filming or striking the set.

It's the medic's job to provide immediate medical attention in case of accidents or illness, and there are hazards everywhere: Electrical wires, props, and machinery litter the soundstage. On location, other dangers appear. There's the risk of moving cars, temporary ramps, or speeding trains. Going on location may entail its own risks—set medics might find themselves out in the middle of the desert, in the middle of the ocean, or in a remote jungle arena.

As in most areas of the entertainment industry—especially in Hollywood—landing your first job as a set medic takes

Wayne Fielder, set medic

Even as a child, Wayne Fielder dreamed of being in the medical profession, but he just didn't have the patience to sit through medical school. Instead, he started out in the restaurant business, training as a chef and eventually buying his own place. But deep inside, he always yearned to be in medicine. At the age of 35, he decided to go for training as an emergency medical technician.

After responding to 911 calls for about nine years, a friend suggested he try his luck as a set medic. "A lot of people don't know this job even exists," he says. "I always kind of wanted to be next to show business, so this was the perfect job for me."

Because set medics are almost all union jobs, it may take a year or two to meet all of the requirements for union membership and actually get called to a job as a set medic. After submitting his resume outlining his medical experience to the motion picture first aid union (IATSE, local 767), he waited. It took a little over a year and a half to get any kind of response.

"You need to schmooze with everyone," Fielder says. "You need be very likeable, very courteous on the set. If they like you, they'll call you more often. You pass out your business cards, and hopefully you'll get called.

"The job is 50 percent skill, 50 percent courtesy," he says. "You'll be with big name actors and actresses. Most of the time you are doing absolutely nothing. You have a walkie-talkie during production, and if they need you for any reason they will call you, so you don't have to sit in one location.

"People use you for a day here, a day there. You establish your own name. Once you make friends, you network with each other and you just continuously bounce work off each other."

It's certainly not like working in an emergency room. "Very rarely is there any trauma," Fielder notes. But there are a lot of perks. "A friend of mine is doing *Pirates of the Caribbean II* with Johnny Depp," Fielder says. "They pay for all his meals, hotel rooms. They'll fly in his family when he goes on location to the Caribbean." Another perk is being able to meet famous directors and actors. "Some are there to work and don't want to be bothered. For the most part, they're happy making $20 million a picture. They know you're there as an hourly employee just trying to do your best."

Still another perk is the salary. There's no doubt that the money is very, very good in this business. In addition to top union wages, if you're called to work as a set medic, you're guaranteed eight hours. If the actor or foreman doesn't show up, you can go home—but you're still paid for eight hours. If you're working on a feature film or program, the company is required to feed you a full meal every six hours. Otherwise, they must pay a meal penalty—adding $12.50 an hour to your wages for every 15 minutes they're late with your lunch. "It's amazing the money they actually throw away," Fielder says. "Many people in Hollywood tend to be very spoiled, but I thank every day I'm blessed with this job. When I started on the ambulance, I was making $6.50 an hour. So I'm really thankful to be doing this."

Fielder just finished working on *Bewitched* "I like to work for three months and then take a month off," he says. "A friend of mine called and offered me 20 episodes of a Nickelodeon

(continues)

time, perseverance, and knowing the right people. Once you've received your EMT, nursing, or medical license and you decide you want to be a set medic, you'll have to spend about $300 to buy your own equipment for basic life support and nonprescription medications. Because most jobs are also union in Hollywood, it may take a year or two to meet all of the requirements for union membership and actually get called to a job as a set medic. Once you're a member of the union, you can either leave your name with your union as an available medic, or you may work as an independent contractor.

Unlike many jobs in the entertainment business, being a set medic is an equal opportunity job—it's just as accessible to

---

(continued)

studio set. It's good if you can get steady work for six months to a year. Usually you do a film or TV show, and when that wraps, you're out of work." However, once you're out of work, you're eligible for unemployment until the next gig comes along.

Basically, working on a movie set is pretty tame. "After doing 911 responses for so many years, I haven't even come close to anything I've seen in the field," he says. "Although there have been some fatalities or serious injuries on some sets." There was, for example, one decapitation on the first *Spider-Man* film. "You might not do anything for six months, but that one time an elderly actor has a heart attack or some electrical worker falls off a scaffolding, you have to be ready for that. You get a lot of allergic reactions, lots of splinters during construction—mostly just first aid."

If there are any life-threatening emergencies, he calls 911. "I can stabilize the patient before the ambulance arrives, but really so far I've not had anything major. But you have to be ready."

In the end, it can be satisfying—and you also get to see your name in lights. "I like to see my name in the credits," he confesses. " I get to meet movie stars. I've always thought that people in the movies seemed untouchable. But they're just people. It's very neat, and … the pay is very good."

The only thing he doesn't like about the job are the hours. "The most I've worked is 19 hours straight through," he says. Still, there can be quite a responsibility. "Sometimes you might be doing a film in the middle of the Mohave desert taking care of a crew in the middle of the summer. It's your responsibility to keep everyone hydrated, to carry electrolyte tablets, provide sunscreen. Whatever the conditions, it might be hot, it might be rainy—you've got to keep them healthy. That's your job. The show must go on.

"I don't sit in my office on the set. I make rounds, I make sure my face is seen. Some people sit in their office and wait to get called, but I make myself known. Because of that, when they see me, they say: 'Oh gosh, my back hurts.' They neglect their health. On the set, you're the doc, the psychiatrist. They neglect themselves and say: 'Can you look at my back, I have a strain… Can you lance this for me?' Then you recommend they see the doctor.

"It's very rewarding. When you wrap, after doing a whole movie, you've bonded with the crew, 15 hours a day—it's your family."

men as women, and any age is fine. You can make yourself even more marketable by getting scuba certification so you can be available during underwater filming, or by getting certified to operate an automatic defibrillator, so you can carry your own device. Getting pediatric certification will allow you to work with infants used in film or TV productions.

Pitfalls

It can be a long, hard slog to break into the business and start getting jobs, and once you do, the hours can be quite long, especially for set medics on location during a movie shoot. Going on location could mean you're away from home for two or three months.

Perks

The pay is top notch and the perks are terrific (lots of great catered food, plenty of snacks, and very little to do most of the time). If you're working on a film, going on location can mean you're sent to a beautiful spot anywhere in the world, with food and lodging paid for. If you're away for several months, the company may pay to fly your family in to visit. If you're a film buff, working on a set with movie stars and famous individuals can be fun as well.

Get a Jump on the Job

In most states you can get your EMT certification at age 18. Get certified in your hometown and go out on calls to see if this is the sort of thing you enjoy. Some areas allow you to become a first aid attendant or ambulance corps volunteer at 14 or 16. Check the various volunteer service organizations in your town to see how you can help, and if this is the type of career in which you might be interested. After clocking a few years as an EMT, you may be ready to try your luck as a set medic.

SOUND MIXER

OVERVIEW

Most people who watch a film never stop to think about the sounds they hear. They take for granted that they're able to hear a conversation over the background noise of traffic, pounding rain or a cheering crowd. They never stop to wonder how it is they can hear every whisper, or that every sound is crisp and smooth.

Those accomplishments in a film or movie are credited to the sound mixer—a person responsible for recording dialogue and sound effects and making sure all the sounds work together. The sound mixer determines which microphones should be used for each scene, and operates the sound recorder. In order to know which microphones are necessary, he or she must have a thorough understanding of the tone of the scene. Sound would be very different in a scene depicting an elderly, sick person in a hospital, for instance, than it would be in a scene depicting a group of children playing outside.

The sound mixer generally is in charge of the sound crew, which usually includes one or more boom operators, a cable person and sometimes—but not always— an equipment technician. In addition to movies, films, and documentaries, sound mixers work in television and sometimes on live performances.

If you land a job as a sound mixer, you'll work closely with the director to determine sound perspective. You'll be the person responsible for making sure the level of sound remains consistent, and that

AT A GLANCE

Salary Range

Pay for sound mixers varies greatly, depending on the employer, location, and experience. An experienced sound mixer working on a feature film can make $500 to $600 a day, plus overtime. However, TV stations and independent film and documentary producers pay less.

Education/Experience

There are no specific educational requirements to become a sound mixer. Many sound mixers start out as boom operators and progress into mixing. However, it's important to understand the properties of sound and technical audio, and some training in sound technology is necessary. Many colleges and some trade schools provide courses in electronic theory, acoustics and other, related fields that would be helpful if you wish to be a sound mixer.

Personal Attributes

You should be energetic and willing to work long hours, and must be able to effectively communicate ideas to others, and to work under production pressure. Openness to adventure and a good sense of humor are desirable.

Requirements

An understanding of sound and a good ear are absolutely necessary. You should be attuned to the properties and complexities of sound.

Outlook

Jobs in the entertainment industry, including sound mixing, are expected to increase by between 10 and 20 percent through the year 2012. That job growth is considered to be average. However, because their numbers are limited, sound mixers are more in demand than some other positions within the industry.

there's no distortion. That means typically keeping a sound report, noting sound levels, microphone settings and other factors in each scene.

You'll need to own your own equipment to make you more marketable—this means you'll earn more money than a mixer without equipment. Necessary equipment varies for different types of work, but you'd need to have some audio equipment and mixing equipment.

Pitfalls

Until you're established as a sound mixer you might have to accept low-paying jobs in order to gain experience and get yourself

---

Anton Gold, sound mixer

The best thing about being a sound mixer, according to 29-year-old Anton Gold, is that his work takes him all over the world. Although he lives in Dorchester, Massachusettes, he's gone from six to nine months of the year. "Travel has been my niche for the past three years," Gold says. During those years, he's worked on films and documentaries in Egypt, Israel, Afghanistan, Chile, Argentina, Turkey, Switzerland, Poland, Italy, Romania, and Canada.

A sound mixer willing to travel—particularly a sound mixer who owns his own equipment and is willing to travel—is a hot commodity, because there's a serious worldwide shortage of people qualified to perform this job. Only the United States, England, and Germany have schools in which you can learn the art of mixing sound, Gold says. Once you're trained and have a little experience, you're sure to be in demand.

"Only those three countries are known for audio mixing," Gold says. "If a production crew wants to do an American-style feature in South America or Africa or Central Asia, there are no sound mixers. They have to bring somebody in. That's why I get a lot of work."

Gold likes working on documentaries more than anything, and has been widely recognized for his work as a sound mixer. Among other awards, Gold received New York University's Best Video Documentary award in 1997 for *Amram Jam*, a film about musician David Amram. However, he says, because documentary work doesn't pay all that much, he supplements his income by working on feature films.

Those include *Lobster Farm*, with Danny Aiello and Jane Curtin in 2004; *The Keeper*, with Maurice Bleibtrau and Vanessa Redgrave in 2003; and *Rent a Husband*, with Brooke Shields and Chevy Chase in 2002.

If you're looking for a high profile, ego-boosting job, sound mixing is not for you, he says. However, sound mixers are very necessary to a production, so you generally are appreciated, which is rewarding.

"Sound mixing isn't a glory job like being the cinematographer or the director," Gold says. "Most sound mixers aren't in it because they want to be widely recognized. But, you work as closely as anyone with actors and actresses—putting mikes under their clothes—you have to be up close and personal. And, you're very necessary to the production, so people sort of look up to you."

Because mixing sound is a specialized skill, Gold says, there normally is no one else on a set who knows how to do your job, which is to make sure that all the different sounds in a scene

(continues)

known in the industry. Some sound mixers are willing to work for meals and industry credits in order to get their names out and gain experience. You can run up considerable debt buying even basic sound mixing equipment.

Perks

Mixing sound is an extremely important part of film and TV production, and sound mixers generally enjoy respect and admiration from the rest of the crew. Sound mixers tend to enjoy their work, despite the challenges and potential for stress.

Get a Jump on the Job

Grab your parents' video camera (be sure to ask first!) and make a movie. Experts say that hands-on experience, regardless of the level, is the best way to learn about sound. If your school does theatrical productions, volunteer to be a sound technician. Experiment with sound in any way you can to get a better idea of the properties and qualities of different sounds.

(continued)

are at their desired level and intensity. "As a sound mixer, nobody else knows what you're doing, so there's nobody looking over your shoulder," Gold says. "Nobody is going to second-guess the sound mixer."

An experienced sound mixer with equipment can earn between $500 and $600 a day while working on a feature film, Gold says. The necessary equipment probably will cost between $50,000 and $75,000. Once the equipment is paid off, Gold says, it's possible to make a good living as a sound mixer.

However, the work is hard, and you've got to be ready for anything. A documentary, for instance, might be filmed primarily outdoors. The location could be in the deserts of Afghanistan, where temperatures soar to close to 100 degrees on a daily basis. Gold, who has worked on documentaries in Afghanistan and other war zones, also has worked in maximum security prisons and has gone undercover with drug dealers. Not all sound mixing occurs on cushy indoor sets, working with famous actors and actresses.

To be an effective sound mixer, you should first learn how to operate a boom microphone, Gold says. There still are many times when he must serve both as boom operator and sound mixer. "You have to have a good ear and you should like audio in general," he says.

While Gold specialized in sound mixing at New York University in New York City, he says it's possible to learn how to mix sound by being an apprentice. However, he says, that would necessitate working without pay for several months at least.

"I'm certainly glad that I was able to do it the way I did, by going to school to specialize in sound mixing," Gold says. "But I've trained other people to do it, so I know that you can get into it that way, too."

While Gold didn't aspire to be a sound mixer when he was very young, he has had a lifelong interest in the entertainment industry. "My dad was a huge movie buff, so I grew up seeing a lot of movies," Gold says. "I grew up with an interest in the entertainment business, which gradually became a strong interest in audio. People don't realize how important sound is, but it's really critical. If you're on an airplane, they don't charge you to watch the movie. They charge you for the headphones so you'll be able to hear the sound."

SPECIAL EFFECTS TECHNICIAN

OVERVIEW

If someone says "special effects," you probably think of the spectacular explosions, killer lightning bolts, car chases, falling buildings, or giant animals that frequently show up in blockbuster movies. Special effect technicians, however, not only work for movie producers, but also for concert promoters, television and radio stations or networks, dance companies, theater and stage companies, and recording studios.

Large, sophisticated productions might require teams of special effects people, while smaller projects might have just one specialist. A special effects technician might work with a special effects coordinator, licensed special effects experts qualified to work with explosives, special effects assistants, and computer graphics specialists. Each of those positions has its own role, but it's the special effects technician who actually creates most of the special effects.

Once the members of a production crew tell the technician the types of effects they're looking for, it's the job of the special effects technician to make them happen. For example, you might be asked to create an alien creature; to add the sounds of thunder and wind to a storm scene; to combine animated characters with live actors (as in the movie *Space Jam*); blow up a car; or to design, set up, and operate mechanical props. You might

be called upon to create rain, snow, and wind; spectacular car crashes; explosions with plumes of smoke; raging skyscraper fires; broken windows; people who have been badly burned or otherwise disfigured; or create miniature cities.

AT A GLANCE

Salary Range

A special effects technician can expect to earn between $40,000 and $80,000 yearly, although salaries vary widely, depending on the type of work, the location, and the type of employer.

Education/Experience

You'll probably be required to have at least a bachelor's degree in broadcasting, theater arts or a related field. An employer also may require several years of practical experience in a related area, or at least an internship in the field of special effects.

Personal Attributes

You should be creative and innovative, and able to quickly put together a Plan B if Plan A doesn't work. In addition, you'll need to be able to communicate your ideas effectively, and have the ability to turn an idea into reality. You should be determined and willing to work long hours.

Requirements

Good mechanical ability is a big plus, as are advanced computer skills and aptitude. Some employers may require union membership. You should have basic carpentry skills. Depending on the type of special effects you do, you may need drawing skills, knowledge of chemicals that enable you to mix formulas or experience with special effects makeup.

Outlook

Special effects technician jobs are expected to increase by between 10 and 20 percent through the year 2012, according to government statistics. That job growth is considered to be average.

Marc Pollack, special effects expert

Marc Pollack has worked as a production manager, property master, and art director, but has found that nothing is as much fun as creating special effects. As president of the special effects company Flix FX, Inc. in North Hollywood, California, Pollack says there are the frustrations of clients who keep changing their minds about what they want, the long hours, and the hard work. But special effects work is . . . well, it's fun.

"Building robots and animatronic creatures is fun, and so is building the very large hydraulic-powered effects rigs," Pollack says. "It's great to see things come to life."

Pollack graduated from the State University of New York's Purchase campus with a BFA in theater arts and film production. His first job was as a production assistant—an entry level job in the entertainment industry. "That job was a means of apprenticing toward the types of work I was interested in," Pollack says.

He started his own Flix FX, Inc. (http://www.flixfx.com) in 1991, and has been busy creating special effects ever since. The company provides mechanical and physical special effects for the advertising and entertainment industries. He and his employees create props and graphics ranging from radio-controlled robots to miniature houses. Their work has appeared on TV, in feature films, commercials, stage shows, store displays, theme parks, museums, and casinos, and chances are very good that you'll recognize some of it.

They've propelled milk and cereal out of an exploding box for Total cereal, created a snow blizzard at a post office for the U.S. Postal Service, and made custom, kid-sized, motorized Jeeps for a Jeep commercial. Their work has appeared on television shows including *Alias*, *Lizzie McGuire*, *The Drew Carey Show*, *Angel*, *Bad Cop*, and *Mad TV*. Featured films in which their special effects have appeared include *Black Hawk Down*, *Men in Black*, and *Mighty Joe Young*.

Creating all these different kinds of special effects can require a variety of skills. Some special effects technicians specialize—you might choose to become an expert in computer-generated effects, make-up, pyrotechnics, or sound—or you can decide to become a jack-of-all-trades. In most cases, it's probably a better idea to learn how to create a variety of effects, so that you'd be prepared to work on as many different projects as possible.

Where and how you work will depend on the type of special effects you're creating. If you're creating computer-generated special effects, for instance, you'll work in a studio, whereas at-the-scene special effects can take you nearly anywhere and everywhere.

Regardless of where you work, however, you'll need to pay very close attention to safety, because creating special effects can be dangerous work.

Pitfalls

Most production work—including special effects—is performed by independent experts or special effects companies, and most of the work goes to people who are already well known within the industry. This means it can be difficult to break into the business. Once you do break in and begin working, there are likely to be days when you'll wonder why you bothered. Special effects work can involve long days spent in uncomfortable conditions. If

There is no such thing as a typical day in the special effects business, Pollack says, but you should know that there will be long days. Special effects for TV commercials generally have to be done within several days to a couple of weeks, which can make for stressful work situations. Still, he says, the rewards are worth it. "The feeling of accomplishment you get when you've built something really cool is great," he says.

While Pollack's educational background is in theater arts and film production, there are a number of areas of study that could be helpful for someone wanting to become a special effects technician. Knowledge of math and physics are valuable to determine forces, measurement, weights, and volumes, as are art and mechanical design and construction.

"There are very many disciplines related to special effects," Pollack says. "Everything from pyrotechnics to postproduction digital effects, and from monsters to models. I would advise you to investigate those disciplines that interest you and then build something. It's a hands-on occupation."

While education is important, Pollack says, you'll also need to have some work to show to prospective employers. He recommends that you build, draw or design a project that you can use to begin a portfolio. It's important to remember that special effects work involves people in many different areas of work, including sculpting, welding, machining, model making, metal fabricating, and computers. "There are so many niches that can be filled," Pollack says.

It's also extremely important to know that the dangerous-looking special effects you see on TV and in movies are created and performed by experienced professionals, he says. He emphasizes that you should never, ever experiment with creating special effects that could hurt someone.

you're creating rain, for instance, you're likely to get wet—and stay wet—for a long time. If you're creating explosions and fire, it's likely to be hot, not to mention dangerous.

Perks

Special effects technicians tend to be a creative lot, and enjoy using that creativity in their work. Most special effects work varies from day to day, which is great if you're not the type of person who's happy sitting at a desk filling out forms or making phone calls.

Get a Jump on the Job

Work on developing your technical and mechanical skills by learning all you can about how computers are used in special effects work and getting good at taking things apart and putting them back together. Once you begin getting some experience, you'll need to put together a good portfolio, keeping track of everything you've done. The next step would be to land a job as an errand-runner for special effects companies or "shops," most of which are in Los Angeles.

STORYBOARD ARTIST

OVERVIEW

Every commercial you see, every action sequence, most films, and most music videos start out as a bunch of sketches on the drawing pad of a storyboard artist.

A storyboard artist is the person hired by the producer to create comic book-style drawings of the movie that filmmakers use to plan how they will visualize a story. A storyboard artist first meets with the director of the film, TV show or TV commercial to find out what shots, camera angles, camera placement, and action are needed. You make notes or do some sketches on the spot, and then go back to your office and draw the shots the director described.

These are usually done in black and white, pencil or pen and ink on paper and drawn within a photocopied rectangle which represents what the camera actually will see in the viewfinder. This way, the producer and director see how the movie will look on paper before the production company goes to the expense of actually making the film. Storyboarding allows stunt performers and special effects experts to see what the director wants so they can be better prepared to do their job for the film. Most artists draw between 15 and 60 drawings a day, depending on the level of detail required.

After a first pass of the entire film, you'll continue to clean up and revise drawn panels, taking direction from the head of story and the director. If your idea of a dream job involves a combination of your artistic skills with the fast-paced

AT A GLANCE

Salary Range

$25,000 to $80,000+ for storyboarding advertising agencies; six-figure salaries for storyboarding a major movie.

Education/Experience

College is not required, but commercial art, illustration, or film production studies can help; a good working understanding of film production and terms and of course the ability to draw are vital.

Personal Attributes

Artistic ability, ability to meet deadlines.

Requirements

Basic computer literacy plus storyboard software; extremely strong pre-visualization and artistic drawing skills—especially a strong ability to handle perspective from many different angles.

Outlook

This job has a high turnover rate but offers a good salary and chance for advancement.

excitement of the entertainment industry, a career as a storyboard artist may be right for you.

Some directors, like Martin Scorsese or Brian De Palma, draw their own storyboards, but others prefer to hire professional illustrators. If there are lots of people, car scenes, stunts or special effects, storyboards are very important, because these scenes can be hard to articulate if you don't see them visually. In a business where every second represents big money, you want people to know how to shoot without wasting much time fussing about what's going to be in the shot.

Some storyboarders are hired to draw just one scene, or to storyboard an entire movie—so a job can be as short as one day or as long as six months. Not only can they show a director what a shot will look like—they also can reveal when you've got too many shots, or if a sequence just isn't important. In order to sketch out a script into a storyboard, the artist must plan camera shots, visualize the story before drawing it, and be careful to maintain continuity among the shots.

Most young artists dream of being an illustrator or a famous painter, but if you

Bill Lyle, storyboard artist

Bill Lyle spent eight years of filmmaking and drawing before he hit the storyboard business—and once he started, he's never looked back. "I was a young kid and I realized I was a good drawer," he says. "Everyone acknowledged me as the best artist in the class, I won a couple of awards along the way. Before you know it, you're thinking you should be an artist. I always liked movies and TV shows. I found the right track on my own."

After attending film school in Victoria, Canada, he worked on his filmmaking skills, making countless shorts, commercials, and what he calls "goofy stuff" for himself, eventually moving on to a classical animation program at Capilano College in North Vancouver, where he began to develop his storyboarding skills. Today, he draws boards for animations, features, and commercials for KitKats, Tylenol, HBO boxing, Juice Box, Reese Puffs, Similac, Bratz dolls, Gorton's seafood, Diet Coke, and many more. He also produces commercials, music videos, and corporate films for entertainment-based clientele.

"I kind of stumbled into storyboarding," he recalls. "I didn't know what it was when I was in film school at age 18. I was thinking about a short film I'd made, and I started drawing pictures about it. I decided to draw what we filmed, after we filmed it. Then I realized it was helping me come up with new ideas."

From that point on, he started storyboarding student projects. Once in animation school, storyboarding was a big component of animation and live action.

There are many different reasons for storyboarding, depending on the project. When doing commercials, storyboarding helps clarify complicated scenes. "You need to plan when you're filming something," he explains. "When you're building a house, you need to draft the plans so you know what you're building. It's the same with a storyboard. When you have your finished storyboard, that's exactly what your shots are going to look like. Once you know it's working on paper, then you can go ahead and make it. You have it scripted, and then storyboarded."

Storyboards are used in animation to help the layout artist who is drawing the background, and in giving other artists direction. Storyboarding also shows animators what the actions are supposed to be.

Even in films, a storyboard helps clarify the process for the whole crew and director, so they all know how things are going to work out. "I've had directors send me a script, and say, 'Storyboard a page of this'—without direction," Lyle says. "I show them how I'm going to do it. But normally, they give you direction and you get a script, you can follow along with what's gong on. "

(continues)

love filmmaking and you draw well, you might want to think about storyboarding. Since it's not so well known, storyboarders are in demand right now. Starting out on this career track as an assistant, you'll typically begin by doing clean-up and revisions, eventually working up to preparing some parts of the storyboard yourself under supervision. This work involves a lot of cutting and pasting, drawing and quick sketching, perspective and composition, and perhaps most importantly, story development and interpretation. Some storyboarders have agents who represent

---

(continued)

Storyboards are also used by writers or directors pitching a movie idea to producers. "You can go into a meeting with storyboards and show the idea to the client," Lyle explains, "how you're going to go about filming something, how the film's opening scene will look." In particular, action movies are heavily storyboarded. "If it's a dull Canadian drama it wouldn't be storyboarded," he laughs, "but big-time movies, all comic-book hero movies like *Spider-Man*—they're all storyboarded."

It makes for quite a lot of drawing. "I've done opening scenes of a movie, the first quarter of a movie, and that was a lot of work!" Lyle says. "I just got 24 episodes of an animated TV show, something like *Shrek*," he says. "That will be lots of work." Commercials, on the other hand, are quick and easy. "For a lot of commercials, I do them overnight, 60 panels in a night, and then have revisions in the morning. "

He gets calls to do storyboarding from all over the world. "They can give me directions over the phone and just send me the script, although a lot of directors like to sit down with you and communicate," he says. "It's a lot cheaper to film in Canada, so a lot of U.S. producers are coming to Vancouver and saving thousands."

Like just about everything in the entertainment business, breaking in to storyboarding is the hardest part. "It's kind of a secret society," Lyle explains. "I had to slowly figure it out. In commercials you have to figure out who the production manager is, and finding that list is tricky." Networking is important, he says. "You've got to have patience, you've got to work hard. A lot of the time you don't get paid at first; when you start out it takes a while to get things moving. Once you pay your dues, things start happening. It's a cool business.

Lyle has agents in New York and Los Angeles, but a lot of his assignments come from people stumbling on his Web site or from local referrals in Vancouver. All in all, Lyle says he likes just about everything about his job. "I like seeing the finished product on TV," he says, "I like getting the call, I like drawing, I like it when people compliment me, and I like telling people about the job.

"When I'm storyboarding, I'm fully in the zone, I'm in the movie, I'm thinking like I'm the camera man, I'm the director. It's cool. The director gives you input, they'll ask you if they're stuck, you get to give them creative feedback. It's pretty cool when the director goes with what you thought. When you see the movie, you think: 'Hey, I came up with that!'"

storyboard artists to different production companies, it can be helpful because they might find you jobs that you couldn't find yourself—but they take 18.5 percent of your profits.

Pitfalls

This is often a difficult career to break into, and once you're there you'll have to deal with constant deadlines with long hours that often bleed into the weekend. Many storyboarders burn out, or become uncomfortable with never knowing what the next job will turn up.

Perks

The money can be extremely good for established storyboarders, and the work is often exciting and intense. It can be enormously satisfying to come up with an alternative idea that the director likes better than the original, watching it acted, filmed and end up in the finished movie.

Get a Jump On the Job

Read as much as you can about film production, and storyboarding, and pay attention to the trade magazines so you know what films are in production. Study videos carefully so you can count the different shots and figure out why a certain shot is used when. Become familiar with Photoshop and computers, because these skills will probably become even more important. Most important, do a lot of life drawing, which is also emphasized in animation schools: Draw figures, draw from life. Draw people and animals moving, doing various things in different locations, and do lots of traditional art; cartooning comes later.

STUDIO TEACHER

OVERVIEW

It may seem as if child stars have it great—hanging around an exciting movie set all day without going to school. But that's not quite the way it works. California, where most child stars live and work, has extremely strict rules about how long a child may act and how much time they must spend studying (three hours out of eight) and even sets minimum grade standards. If a child star gets below a C in any subject, their entertainment working papers can be pulled. So school can be serious business for these young stars.

Because California has such strict rules, there are lots of job openings for studio teachers, who act not just as an instructor, but also as a sort of welfare monitor. In California, any entertainment-related projects involving children—movie sets, commercial shoots, even still-photography sessions—must have child welfare minders and instructors on the premises. This means you'll find teachers on commercials, photo shoots, TV pilots, music videos—even voice-overs for cartoons. For every 10 professional child stars, a studio must hire one studio teacher.

If the child actor normally attends a regular school and is only acting on the side, the studio teacher must work with the child's regular teachers to make sure the child's grades don't suffer. All child actors must follow those rules until they turn 18 or get their GED.

California state law requires that teachers who work on entertainment industry

AT A GLANCE

Salary Range

About $300 a day for as little as three hours of work. Salary varies according to whether the show is union, overtime, and so on.

Education/Experience

In California, studio teachers must have a valid studio teacher's certificate and be certified. You should be skilled in teaching one or more academic subjects with experience working with students one-on-one or in small groups. Multisubject capability is a great advantage, as is the ability to teach a foreign language.

Personal Attributes

Flexible, easygoing, pleasant, enjoy kids.

Requirements

A studio teacher must hold dual teaching certification in California: a California Multiple Subject credential (elementary school) and a Single Subject Credential (high school). In addition, the studio teacher must hold a Studio Teacher Credential issued by the California Department of Labor. This credential denotes a thorough knowledge of California child labor laws, including the rules governing the number of hours child actors can be on set and how that time can be spent.

Outlook

Excellent. With new California credentialing laws, the number of accredited studio teachers plummeted, making lots of room for new teachers.

sets (film, theater, TV, etc.) hold a special California Studio Teacher Certification. According to California law, the studio teacher, in addition to teaching, also has the responsibility of watching out for the health, safety, and morals of child actors under age 16. This might mean they can do anything from asking the director not to swear around the kids to monitoring how much junk food they scarf down at the snack table. The studio teacher is also there to protect their employer (the movie company) from legal issues related to working with children.

Most nonunion studio teachers (which you'll be when you start out) sign up with agencies that send you out on work and take a commission of between 20 and 35 percent. Union teachers aren't allowed to have an agency; instead, they get work directly through the union. If you land a job as a studio teacher, you'll be expected to be able to handle teaching children from ages 2 to 18. Below high school level, you'll need to be able to teach all subjects, but once the student reaches high-level math or languages, even the most experienced teacher may need to turn to other tutors for a long-term job. This usually comes out of the studio budget.

Typically, in the beginning a studio teacher handles just single day jobs, and the

Lucas Moore, studio teacher

Lucas Moore has worked with child actors on some of the top shows in Hollywood, but at heart he's a teacher who cares passionately about his kids and about education. He's been known to sternly correct a production assistant who tells a young actor that he has to go to school now. "Don't ever say that again," he'll admonish. "School is not a punishment—something you have to get out of the way in order to have fun!"

Competent in Spanish and French, Lucas Moore has a master's degree in secondary education from Georgia State University and is a certified studio teacher who's worked with kids in film, TV, industrials, theater, and commercials. He maintains the child's studies while supervising the education, welfare, and well being of kids working in the business.

As a Georgia schoolteacher who had studied acting and directing in college, he used to moonlight as a stagehand. When the movie *Pet Sematary II* came to town, he was hired to work as a studio teacher with young extras—and it just continued from there, taking him around the world with his young charges who were working on projects including *7th Heaven*, *Melrose Place*, *Joan of Arcadia*, *Nick Freno*, *Little Boy Blue*, *The Santa Clause*, *The Jungle Book*, *The Big Green*, *The Burning Season*, *The Monroes*, *Summer of Fear*, *Return to Lonesome Dove*, *White Oleander*, and *Sabrina—the Teenage Witch*.

In general, he doesn't have too much trouble with disciplinary problems because child actors tend to be bright and creative. Those with strong family support, he says, do very well with on set schooling and go on to have successful college careers: Fred Savage (*The Wonder Years*) and his brother Ben (*Boy Meets World*) both went on to Stanford University; Jonathan Taylor Thomas (*Home Improvement*) is studying at Harvard; Jodie Foster graduated from Yale; Brooke Shields graduated from Princeton.

Moore says he prefers the independence of studio teaching, compared to the situation in public schools. "But it's a two-edged sword," he notes. "I do get to make certain decisions—I don't have to worry about bureaucracy. But I don't have a support system. The producer has other things to care about."

(continues)

student returns to their regular school the next day after completing their homework under the studio teacher's supervision. The teacher makes sure the child actor isn't on the set a minute more than they are legally allowed to be. (For example, a six-year-old actor can be on set for no more than eight hours.) During that time, the child must have three hours of education, one hour of rest/recreation, and one hour of meal time, leaving just three hours for filming a day.

Typically, you'll either teach on a full-day or hourly basis. For a day project, you must be on set for a full day (typically nine hours, including meal break), and you're paid a flat day rate. For an hourly project, you'd be on set only for a specific block of hours (usually three or less), and you'd be paid an hourly rate.

Studio teachers must monitor all requirements, and work closely with the assistant director to make sure those requirements are satisfied. The laws regarding the tutoring of children in the entertainment fields are often stricter than with ordinary home schooling. The studio teacher is there, first and foremost, as a defense against the business forces that would overwork and jeopardize child actors. Studio teachers are sometimes the

(continued)

It can sometimes be stressful on a set. "It's not unusual to get just 20 minutes worth of school at a time," he notes. "It's not unusual to have a production assistant stand by the door counting the minutes." Other times, he notes, the child star resists going back to work and just wants to stay in the schoolroom, working on a project. "These kids tend to be bright. Although they do have charisma—they're still just kids. School is a refuge for them." There have been times, he says, when a production assistant comes knocking on the door to retrieve the child for the next scene, and the actor says "Go away! I'm not ready."

"I will often turn down low budget films," he says, "because they try to cut corners and try to get you to look the other way" when it comes to child labor laws.

Moore enjoys all aspects of his job, but notes that he—and most studio teachers—prefer working movies, because you work a number of months and then you can take a break before going on to the next project. Working on a series, you must work 10 months or longer at a stretch. In a town that thrives on "What have you done lately" and "Who do you know," working on a series takes you out of circulation, and people forget about you.

If you think you'd like teaching and you're attracted to Los Angeles and the movies, Moore recommends that you first get a few years of experience teaching in traditional schools. "You need to learn how it works, how children relate to each other," he explains, before hanging out your shingle as a Hollywood studio teacher. "I will admit that in late September, I drive by a school and see the teachers cars parked outside as they prepare, and I miss my classroom. But I don't miss the bureaucracy. I think studio teaching is wonderful, and I'll retire doing this."

sole advocate for the well-being of the child actor.

Pitfalls

There can be political issues in the tug-of-war over the best interests of the child, for whom the studio teacher is being paid to protect; the production company, who pays the studio teacher and the child's agent or manager (who sometimes doesn't mind bending the rules if it makes a producer happy); and the child's parents. Hours can be long and you may need to work weekends or holidays.

Perks

The salary is terrific and the hours are flexible; you can tell your agency the days you want to work and those you don't. And unlike your compatriots in the public schools, you'll probably only have one or two students to monitor. There's also plenty of variety and interest in this job; you also may travel to incredibly exciting places. The more influential child stars have enough power that they can recruit their own traveling teachers, who follow the child actor from place to place, no matter where that leads.

Get a Jump on the Job

If your high school has a "future teachers of America" club, you could consider joining. Consider signing up as a tutor in your school, either working with younger kids in your district or working after school with disadvantaged youngsters or kids who don't speak English. Do a lot of baby-sitting, too, so you get used to working with kids.

STUNT PERFORMER

OVERVIEW

Stunt performers are hired to perform acts that are too dangerous for an actor, or which the actor doesn't have the expertise to perform. Stunt performers drive speeding cars, fly planes, fall down flights of stairs, fight, interact with animals, leap from tall buildings, and jump over barriers in commercials, movies, and TV shows.

Performing stunts, however, doesn't mean you have to be crazy or take unnecessary risks. To the contrary, there is sometimes real risk involved, stunt performers must behave cautiously, perform their work seriously, and look out for other people on the set.

Most stunt performers have one or more areas in which they excel, such as martial arts, gymnastics, boxing, rock climbing, or skateboarding. While it helps to have a specialty skill and general acting talent, you'll still need to be well rounded and a team player. Stunt coordinators hire stunt performers for particular jobs and look for individuals who can follow instructions, are cooperative, and want to work as part of a team—not be the star of the show.

There are no specific requirements or training paths for stunt performers. Some work as actors before getting into stunt work, while others attend schools that teach students to perform stunts. A problem for many beginning stunt performers is that you usually need to belong to an actor's union before you can get a job— but you can't get into one of the unions until you've had some experience.

AT A GLANCE

Salary Range

Salaries of stunt performers, also known as stuntmen and stuntwomen, range from less than $5,000 to more than $100,000 a year, depending on factors such as the frequency of work, amount of risk involved, the location of the job, and how widely recognized the stuntperson is. Well-known, experienced stunt performers may be able to name their price, while someone just starting out may work for very little, just to gain the experience.

Education/Experience

There are several schools in the United States that train stunt performers. While these schools can teach you skills and provide information that might make it easier for you to break into stunt work, there are no specific educational requirements for stunt performers. Some stunt performers work as regular actors to start, and then move into stunts.

Personal Attributes

While there are some risks involved with stunt work, a stunt performer must be reasonable and cautious, not reckless or a daredevil. Stunt coordinators stay away from reckless show offs, who they say are more likely to get injured or cause someone else to be injured than someone who is in control. You should be assertive and willing to fight for jobs, for which there often is keen competition. A top-notch level of physical fitness also is necessary. You should have a high level of determination and a willingness to try new things and to push yourself to previously unattained goals.

Requirements

You'll need to have some acting talent, along with some kind of specialized training and experience, whether in gymnastics, operating a motorcycle, martial arts, or whatever. An ongoing level of training is necessary in order to become a stuntperson.

(continues)

AT A GLANCE *(continued)*

Outlook

Jobs in stunt performing are expected to increase by between 10 and 20 percent through the year 2012. That job growth is considered to be average. As with many jobs in the entertainment field, those for stunt performers are very competitive.

The way around that tricky situation is to sign up as an extra on a set. Look for a casting director in your area (not all casting directors live in New York or Los Angeles) and inquire about working as an extra for a union production. If there are parts for extras available and you get the job, you can get an extra's voucher at the end of the shooting day. Once you've accumulated three vouchers, you'll be eligible for union

Manny Siverio, stunt performer/stunt coordinator

Manny Siverio wanted to be in films since he was a little boy growing up in Puerto Rico. Along with the other kids in his neighborhood, he'd reenact the fight scenes they'd see in movies and TV, dreaming to himself of the day that he'd be in showbiz. "I never told anyone that I wanted to be in the film industry because they would have looked at me like I have two heads," Siverio says. "But I knew it was what I wanted to do, and I never gave up my dream."

Now, at age 45, Siverio has performed in or coordinated stunts for more than 200 TV and film productions, including *Dead Presidents*, *The First Wives Club*, *Men in Black*, *Copland*, *Blade*, *New York Undercover*, *Law and Order*, and *The Sopranos*. He's been set on fire, tossed out of high buildings, and hit by cars—all in a day's work. He's doubled for actors Johnny Depp, Joe Pesci, and Michael DeLorenzo, and he's written two books about training for martial arts. He's also an accomplished mambo dancer.

Although he does more coordinating of stunts and stunt performers these days than performing, he's not out of the picture completely. "I can still jump in front of the camera and do my thing," Siverio says.

His start in stunt work came in 1982, when a friend told him about a stunt coordinator who was looking for a young Hispanic guy who could box. Meeting all the qualifications, Siverio landed the job. "That was luck, pure and simple," he says. "I was everything they needed for that project, and I was available."

That enabled him to get a union card—and more jobs. "At first I'd use my ethnicity to get work," he says. "I'm Hispanic, but I can look Italian, or Arab or whatever. But then I got away from that. I didn't want people to look at me as a Hispanic stuntman. I wanted to be known as a stuntman who happens to be Hispanic."

By working hard and establishing many contacts and relationships, Siverio built up a solid reputation. He became known as a stunt performer who was always willing to go the extra mile, such as the time he finished a stunt scene despite significant pain from a motorcycle accident. He traveled whenever necessary, never complained about long, tiring days, and cooperated with others on the set. Once his reputation was established, work began coming to him.

(continues)

membership. The other way to join a union, such as the Screen Actors Guild (SAG) or the American Federation of Television and Radio Artists (AFTRA), is to get "waived in." This occurs on rare occasions when there is no union person available to play a part for which a nonunion person has the exact skills and appearance necessary, and is available to work.

Getting into acting of any kind requires a good deal of luck and being at the right place at the right time. However, good training and determination to succeed also are important. If you have a special skill, such as gymnastics or skateboarding, keep working to develop it. But don't concentrate on just one skill and not bother to broaden your abilities by learning new skills, because it's important to be well rounded. Every skill you master will help when you're looking for work.

Pitfalls

Getting work as a stunt performer is difficult until you've gained some experience

---

(continued)

"I've been very fortunate," Siverio says. "Let's just say that I don't have to send out my head shots anymore."

Siverio has a long background in martial arts, beginning when he was about 10 years old. That training was invaluable, he says, because it developed his skills and agility for stunt work. However, he warns that you can't depend on one skill to launch you into stunt work. And, if it does, it won't assure that you stay working. "Once you're in the door, you need to expand your skills," he says.

He recommends starting out slowly, setting goals for yourself, and working step by step. For instance, you might concentrate on getting a part as an extra, or meeting a stunt coordinator, rather than setting a goal to be a stunt performer in a major film production. "If you try to do it all at once you might fall on your face, get discouraged, and walk away," Siverio says. "Being in the film industry requires a lot of patience and perseverance. It might take years to get your first job."

Stunt coordinators look for team players, not hotshots, Siverio says. And, reputations—both good and bad—spread very quickly among stunt producers. "Besides being talented, you have to know how to follow directions and work as a member of a team," he says. "You can't be a hot-dogger. When you get onto a set, keep your mouth shut and your eyes open, and just listen and learn."

It's important to have a complete resume and a head-and-shoulders photograph of yourself when you begin looking for work. First impressions are very important, Siverio says, so be sure to have the photo taken professionally and have a resume that's complete and nicely done.

Breaking into stunt work isn't easy, nor is working in the field. However, Siverio says, if it's what you want to do, don't give up. "If you have a dream to do something, then go ahead and do it," he says. "You shouldn't let anyone step in the way of dreams. Being a stunt guy isn't for everyone, and I'll tell you that it's hard. But there's nothing much better, as far as I'm concerned."

and established a solid reputation. You'll probably need to have another job to provide supplementary income at first, but you'll need to find a job with a schedule that's flexible enough to allow you to pursue acting work. When you do get work as a stuntperson, you may be required to travel for extended periods of time. Stunt performers normally have fairly short careers because doing stunt work is so physically demanding. While it sounds glamorous, filming shows and movies is hard work, normally requiring very long hours and little free time.

Perks

Once you're established as a dependable, serious stunt performer, you'll probably have no trouble getting work. Assuming that you work hard and do a great job, a stunt coordinator is likely to tap you for one job after another because the coordinator knows that you're dependable. Stunt performers get to meet all sorts of actors (especially when they double for them) and get to travel on location during filming. Stunt performers who are well known and established can make a lot of money, and normally can work as stunt coordinators when they no longer want to perform.

Get a Jump on the Job

Work hard to develop a specific skill or talent. You'll need a resume when you begin looking for work, so start thinking now about what you might include on it. Make lists of the competitions in which you've participated, noting awards you've received. Take up new sports and ventures and try everything you can. Just be sure that you get adequate instruction before you try something new, and follow all safety guidelines.

VENTRILOQUIST

OVERVIEW

Up there on stage, it's just a ventriloquist and a wooden dummy—but the very best performers can captivate an audience with a combination of voice-controlled skill and terrific jokes.

Ventriloquism is all about illusion—the ventriloquist is trying to direct your attention away from his mouth to the puppet, at the same time using humor to cover missing letters. (With luck, you'll be so busy laughing you won't hear a missing letter). And since there are very few letters you can say without using your mouth at all, the ventriloquist concentrates on those that don't require lip movements (vowels) and makes letter substitutions to skip the most troublesome letters (B, F, M, P, Q, V, and W)—so you'd say "d" instead of "b," for example. If you're sitting in the audience, the ventriloquist will speak quickly and substitute letters, and your brain will automatically fill in the missing spots. This works even better if the ventriloquist has already used the troublesome word, getting your brain ready to hear the word again from the puppet. The other trick ventriloquists use is to substitute easy words for trickier words to say, so that the word "difficult" (tricky to say because of the "f") becomes "hard"—much easier to say without moving the lips.

Next, the ventriloquist practices the sound substitutions until they become automatic. You could practice by reciting poems you know by heart until you can do the substitutions perfectly. You'd say the line first as yourself, and then in the voice of the puppet. You'll need to get to the

> ## AT A GLANCE
>
> ### Salary Range
> Incredibly varied, from a beginner's $100 per job to the top comedic performer's "sky's the limit" salary.
>
> ### Education/Experience
> Experience in comedy; no particular education required.
>
> ### Personal Attributes
> Engaging personality, good stage presence, patience, and a good sense of humor.
>
> ### Requirements
> Talent at ventriloquism, comedic skills, ability to work hard, and good communication skills.
>
> ### Outlook
> Fair; there are very few ventriloquists working in this country, so success is possible for those willing to work very hard.

point where you can change automatically, quickly and smoothly from your voice to the puppet voice and back again.

Ventriloquists also spend time training their voice and learning how to breathe properly (most people breathe incorrectly, from their stomach and not from their diaphragm). Once you obtain your puppet, you must practice in front of a mirror so that your dialogue (typically about 15 minutes long) is fast and effortless—and don't forget puppet movements! You'll also need to work on moving the parts of the puppet so its reactions seem normal and human-like.

Once you've perfected your voice control, you'll need to find a dummy (lots of good places on the Internet) you can use on stage as your alter ego. As you improve, you can add new "characters"—but each one must be distinctive, not just in looks

Jeff Dunham, ventriloquist

Jeff Dunham has been working with dummies since he was in elementary school, and he's loved every minute of it. "I was one of those lucky people who found something very early in life that I loved doing," he says. "I had a lot of fun. Ventriloquism is unique—not many other people at all were doing it, and being a shy kid, it enabled me to have another voice. I could hide behind the dummies. I wasn't really saying things—it was the dummy!" The stage work gave him confidence, recognition, and some measure of fame.

Although the idea of being a ventriloquist is sometimes a joke in this culture— "kind of like someone who plays the accordion," he says—his skill has earned him respect and attention, even in the beginning. "Kids are sometimes cruel," he says, "and you might think a ventriloquist would get made fun of, but all the way through high school and college it was the exact opposite. The recognition I got when I came out for talent shows was great. My parents and my friends were all supportive, and it was plain old fun. Why in the world would I ever quit?"

Praised for his hilarious comedy routines, his great personality and ventriloquist ability, the thirty-something veteran performs 40 weeks a year in concert venues and comedy clubs. One of the hardest working entertainers around, he's the only person ever to win the prestigious "Ventriloquist of the Year" Award twice. He also was recently nominated "Comedian of the Year" by the INN Music City News Country Awards, and has appeared on *The Tonight Show* more than any other ventriloquist—five times with Johnny Carson, seven times with Jay Leno. In fact, Dunham is proudest of the fact that Johnny Carson invited him to the couch on his very first *Tonight Show* appearance, an honor Jeff shares with only four other comedians during Carson's 30-year tenure.

He started performing at age seven in his native Dallas, Texas, when—as a way to overcome his shyness—he invented a crowd of characters who could talk for him. He taught himself ventriloquism using a plastic Mortimer Snerd puppet, a few books and records, and put on his first show by the time he was in third grade. At first he earned the equivalent of $5 (about $50 in today's money) and by age 12 he was handling corporate gigs for the likes of the Kiwanis Club. By age 13 he was audited by the IRS. He studied communications at Baylor University while continuing working around the country, getting paid so well he was able to buy his own car with the proceeds.

(continues)

but in personality and voice. The more different from the way you look and sound, the better. Then you need to go out there and start getting engagements, starting out small and working your way up to larger venues. Try out for talent competitions and don't stop working—eventually, if you're good enough, you can attract an agent and start doing bigger shows, perhaps thinking about TV appearances.

Pitfalls

It can be tough to make a living at first, and you may have to work some shows for free. People don't always treat ventriloquists with respect, because there are many substandard ventriloquists out there. Moreover, modern special effects technology has made many audiences less appreciative of the skill at throwing the voice.

(continued)

When he won a college talent competition in the early 1980s, one of the judges was an agent from William Morris agency, who signed Dunham immediately. "Timing is everything," he says. "It's been a wonderful journey working very hard, very hard, but being ready when opportunity came by."

He moved to Los Angeles in 1988 to work on beefing up his comedy act at the Improv and the Comedy & Magic. With his first *Tonight Show* spot in April 1990, his career took off. He has since appeared regularly on *The Tonight Show* and in specials like *Country Nights*, as well as performing as the headliner at concerts across the country. He also toured with the Broadway musical *Sugar Babies*, and has been the opening act for Gloria Estefan, Julio Iglesias, Reba McEntire, Glen Campbell, Tanya Tucker, the Oakridge Boys, and Bob Hope.

As he worked on his ventriloquism, his comedy routines gradually improved as well. "I don't think you have enough life experience to draw on to do heartfelt comedy performance until you're at least in your late 20s," he says. "To create your own unique comedy, that's what takes the time and skills and hours onstage. At a young age it's great to get script books and get others to write for you. Early on I was more a ventriloquist who was piecing together the comedy. Now the ventriloquism is a vehicle for my comedy—a way of presenting my own twisted jokes." His puppet costars include the oversized Jose Jalapeno on a Stick; Peanut, a purple potbellied "woozle"; and Walter, a grumpy baldy with a permanent frown. Dunham's other characters include a gorilla, a cockroach, and a worm at the bottom of a tequila bottle.

What Dunham particularly enjoys is working on new characters. "I'm me on stage, but I'm creating other characters in these dummies," he says. "They can say things I can never get away with."

If you've ever thought the ventriloquist's life is for you, Dunham warns that you need to develop an act, not just the ability to throw your voice, if you want to be successful. "Too many people who want to be a ventriloquist tend to rely on just the skills of making a dummy talk," he says. "If you only learn the skills of a ventriloquist, all you have is the tools for creating comedy. But you haven't learned how to be funny, and that's the most important part. It's like learning to juggle," Dunham says. "Anybody can learn to juggle, but to come up with an act where you can entertain people for a half an hour—that's something else."

Perks

If you're creative with a great sense of humor and the ability to carry a room, this job can be incredibly exciting and lead to all sorts of entertainment gigs all over the world.

Get a Jump on the Job

Get a good ventriloquism videotape (and a dummy!) and practice, practice, practice. The most important thing is to get onstage in front of people and do as many shows as you can, at nursing homes, at school (even giving book reports or oral presentations can help), at local service organizations such as the Kiwanis—no matter how big the crowd, 10 people or 1,000. The only way you can improve is to have that experience. Hire yourself out to birthday parties. Consider attending the annual ventriloquist convention (http://www.venthaven.com) held every summer in Fort Mitchell, Kentucky.

VOICE-OVER ARTIST

OVERVIEW

Whether it's the Latin silky smooth voice of Puss 'n Boots in *Shrek II*, the sweet innocence of *Bambi*, or the menacing tones of Cruella de Vil in Disney's *101 Dalmations*, the voices of animated characters, along with the unseen narrators of TV and radio commercials and the soothing sound of radio talk, are all brought to life by voice-over artists. They're also often used by ad agencies to do promotions, documentaries, film narrations, and much more.

Success as a voice-over actor is more than just having an interesting voice—you have to breathe life and soul into a two-dimensional character. Doing voice-over work is one of the purest forms of acting, because your whole being is focused through your voice alone.

If you think this sounds like an interesting way to make a living, you'll need to take the time to hone your technique and explore your creative range. Don't be surprised if you'll need to devote a good six months to a year to develop your craft. You need to train your voice, do breathing exercises, or take singing lessons to help you learn how to speak and breathe correctly. Read out loud for an hour a day, assuming the personality of the characters you're reading. Don't just recite—*become* the characters.

Next, you should find a good voice-over teacher who can teach you how to market yourself, how to conjure up a host of different characters' voices, and how to sustain them over 10 pages of emotional

AT A GLANCE

Salary Range

$100 to $500 to voice a commercial, doing four to six commercials a day.

Education/Experience

Formal training in broadcasting from a college or broadcasting school is valuable. Most voice-over artists have a bachelor's degree in communications, broadcasting, or journalism. College broadcasting programs offer courses, such as voice and diction, to help students improve their vocal qualities.

Personal Attributes

The most successful voice-over artists attract attention by combining a pleasing personality and voice with an appealing style.

Requirements

Must have a pleasant and well-controlled voice, good timing, excellent pronunciation, and correct grammar.

Outlook

Competition for jobs as voice-over artists will be keen because the broadcasting field attracts many more job seekers than there are jobs. Employment is expected to decline through 2012.

script. Through beginning, intermediate, and advanced classes, a teacher will direct you on how to perform for your demo tape, for auditions, and in front of agents and casting directors. Any city that has voice jobs probably has voice teachers. But you could also get some benefit from plain acting classes—even if they don't specialize in the voice, if they focus on improvisational comedy, dialects, or cold reading. What you want is to have someone challenge you and give you feedback. After you've reached some level of skill and comfort in creating voices, you'll need to create a demo tape, which can cost between $500 and $4,000. Don't skimp here—the demo tape will help you to find an agent, and the agent will help you find work. Make sure it showcases your best work—if an agent isn't impressed in the first 20 seconds, you've probably lost out. Send it to as many agencies as you can find. It's the agent's job to connect you with the person doing the hiring on a voice-over project—a casting director and a voice director, the client (in a commercial) or the advertising agency.

John Peace, voice-over artist

John Peace was pretty much born in a radio station studio, and spent the first half of his life making a living there. "My parents owned the radio station, and I was literally toddling around the station since I was in diapers," Peace recalls. He started officially working at the station at age nine, and right away he knew he wanted to work there. The school bus would drop young John off at the radio station at 3 p.m., where he'd work until dark. Everything he knows about voice-overs, recording, and the business, he learned at his dad's radio station. "It's all been on-the-job training," he says. "I never took a journalism course."

Eventually, however, he got tired of the politics of the radio station. "It's a backstabbing dog-eat-dog world," he says. "The hours are grueling, the benefits are minimal, and the pay isn't that great, either." He'd had a recording studio in his home for some time, where he'd been creating voice-overs for commercials on the side for friends for years. "Eventually, I found I had more work on the side than in the radio station. When I realized it was costing me money to leave my recording studio at the house and go to the station to work, I left the station."

Peace owns his own voice-over production company (Audio Production Experts, http://www.ape.com) and has a stable of 176 voice-over artists. He creates commercials for 75 different agencies. APE talents are featured in national campaigns for such corporations as Denny's, Blockbuster, Hasbro, Disney, Caterpillar, Time-Warner, McDonalds, and Sony.

Peace acts as an agent for the "voice talents" who send him a demo; if he likes what he hears and they're available, he'll put them in his roster. Clients then e-mail Peace a script, explain what they want, and Peace produces it using one of his voice-over artists, and sends it back. If the client is in a hurry, Peace can e-mail a production-quality recording. "We do commercials, TV, and radio all over the United States and some in Canada," he says. Although Peace's company has several offices in the United States, thanks to the Internet they have clients all over the world. Peace can put everything together and send them back an MP3 file, or link up a codex via an ISBN line, and record in real time with studio broadcast quality.

If you want to start out in voice-overs, you have to pay your dues and be patient, Peace says, because success isn't going to happen overnight. "I started when I was 9, and it was only in the last 10 or 15 years that everything came to fruition for me," he says. "You have to set your sights on a goal. If you think you sound good, you can always get better. The number one thing is—don't try to sound like a radio announcer," Peace says.

"It's a fun business, but you'll be tied down to a studio," he says. "If you have to be out and about, this wouldn't be a good job for you." What he likes best, he says, is that he doesn't have just one boss, so he can't make everybody mad and lose all his work. "With so many different clients, there's very good job security," he says.

On a cartoon show, it may be a producer or a studio head. Occasionally, writers and directors may get a say in choosing a voice-over actor. What your agent must do is get those people to decide you're the right person for the role, so he or she will send you out on a couple of auditions to see how you do.

Pitfalls

Voice-over commercial work can be tough to break into; you've got to start small and work your way up, and it can take years to get established. Voice-over acting—those who voice characters for animation films—is even more competitive. Many voice-over artists handle voice-over work through advertising agencies while making their living working as an on-air personality within the broadcast industry. Also, you've got to go where the work is—cartoon voice-overs are mostly in Los Angeles, with a bit in Canada (Vancouver or Toronto). It's also tough getting an agent; top voice agents receive several thousand submissions from novices and accept just one or two a year as new clients.

Perks

If you have a great voice with a lot of warmth and personality, and you enjoy using it, this can be a very fulfilling career with an excellent salary for those who are successful. As a freelance voice-over artist, you can set your own hours and be in charge of your own career.

Get a Jump on the Job

Paid or unpaid internships provide students with hands-on training and the chance to establish contacts in the industry. One of the best places to intern is at a radio station. At a radio station, you can learn the basics of how to make quality recordings. Visit newsstands, specialty bookstores, coffee shops, theaters, and recording facilities looking for fliers, magazines, or newspapers advertising jobs for voice-over actors. Or call local recording facilities, radio stations, animation studios, and traditional acting schools and workshops to learn about workshops or internships. Check out schools that can help you develop voice talent, primarily in California or New York.

Broadcast journalism is an excellent major for those interested in voice-over work, while studying acting can teach you how to interject emotion into your voice. Studying music, whether singing or playing an instrument, can help because timing is so important in making radio commercials.

WARDROBE ASSISTANT

OVERVIEW

From Johnny Depp's tall black hat in *Charlie and the Chocolate Factory* to his pirate getup in *Pirates of the Caribbean*, the actor's appearance was an important part of the *look* of each of these movies. But how an actor looks doesn't happen by accident—and a big part of getting the right clothes is the wardrobe assistant.

Often overlooked and underappreciated, wardrobe assistants work in all types of settings, from theater productions and TV shows to rodeo performances and traveling circuses. Although traveling with a circus is certainly much different from helping with wardrobe for a live theater production, the work of a wardrobe assistant in each of those settings would be similar. Much of the responsibility of making sure the actors and actresses look good falls on wardrobe assistants.

There are two categories of wardrobe assistants—those who work on making the costumes, and those who work with the costumes once they've been designed and sewn. A wardrobe assistant normally would organize and size costumes for each cast member, making sure everything the performers need is ready and in place. If the show travels, as with a circus, the wardrobe assistant would help with packing up and unpacking the costumes. Wardrobe assistants make sure that all costumes remain clean, intact, and in good condition for the shows, help with costume fittings, and alter costumes for

AT A GLANCE

Salary Range

A wardrobe assistant can expect to earn between $10 and $15 an hour, depending on the location of the position, experience required, size of cast, and other factors.

Education/Experience

There is no particular experience necessary to be a wardrobe assistant. Some employers, however, may prefer that you've taken some sewing, textile, or design-related courses.

Personal Attributes

You must be able to communicate effectively with other members of the production crew, as well as the performers. You need to understand fabric, color, and lighting to be able to visualize how a costume will look in a particular scene. Keen vision (especially color vision) is important, as is a moderate degree of physical agility. You'll also need to be willing to take orders, and you should be able to complete tasks without constant supervision.

Requirements

Must have a basic mastery of sewing and be able to operate a sewing machine. Must be familiar with fabrics of all kinds and know how to maintain them. Wardrobe assistants often are required to transport costumes, so a valid driver's license may be necessary.

Outlook

Wardrobe assistant jobs are expected to increase by between 10 and 20 percent through the year 2012. That job growth is considered to be average, according to government statistics.

new cast members. He or she also may be required to help performers in their dressing rooms.

Some wardrobe assistants actually help make costumes, and if you take this job, you may be required to locate and keep track of accessories such as shoes, belts, hats, and gloves, making sure each actor has everything that goes with the costume. Other responsibilities could include altering costumes to fit actors, cutting out costume patterns, and helping to research period costumes.

Nafeesa Saboor, wardrobe assistant

Nafeesa Saboor enjoys working as a wardrobe assistant, but she warns that it's not the most glamorous job in the entertainment industry. In fact, she says, the job entails a lot of mundane tasks and doing favors for the principal stylist, photographers, and others. "Mostly, my job is to satisfy any and all needs of the principal stylist and other people on set for the shoot," she says. "Sometimes that means running to the store for water or supplies. Other times that means steaming garments, holding pins, helping models or actresses put on clothes, or organizing samples."

Still, she says, the position has its good side. "Sometimes I get to offer my input on accessories or go out on buys with the stylist," Saboor says. "Those are the fun parts of the job."

Saboor, who holds a bachelor's degree in English from Spelman College in Atlanta, works as a wardrobe assistant on a freelance basis in New York City and is the administrative assistant to the chief executive officer of hip-hop magazine, as well. It would be difficult, she says, to earn enough to live in New York City without the full-time job, and it's not always easy to find work as a freelance wardrobe assistant.

Mostly, she says, she networks to locate work, keeping in touch with friends and acquaintances who can refer her to stylists and job possibilities. Some of her friends are models who can steer her toward jobs, and Saboor also looks for work opportunities on fashion and entertainment industry Web sites.

She got her start in wardrobe work during an internship with a jeans and apparel company in Atlanta. It was her job to style samples of the clothing for photos that were displayed on the company's Web site. Saboor found out that she enjoyed working with clothing, and decided to pursue wardrobe work after moving to New York City. She has worked on stage productions and with fashion shows, helping to prepare costumes and clothing for the show or presentation. She steams clothing, sews, assists those trying on costumes, organizes costumes, and checks costumes to make sure they're clean.

The only thing typical of a day as a wardrobe assistant, Saboor says, is that you can count on it being long and often tedious. When you're working on a show or production, she says, you normally have to be there by 9 a.m., and the day may not end until 7 p.m. Breakfast and lunch often are provided. During those long days, she says, nerves tend to fray and tempers get short. The trick is to not take it personally.

A good way to get started as a wardrobe assistant is to practice putting together costumes, Saboor advises. You can use your own clothing, your friends' clothing, or you can make clothing. It's important if you want to work in wardrobe to know how to sew and how to steam

Above all, wardrobe assistants need to be able to follow instructions. Production people, including those in wardrobe, often work in stressful conditions, and therefore rely on assistants to follow instructions and complete tasks as requested. Assistants are expected to show up for work on time, meet deadlines, and work long hours as needed.

That's not to say that working as a wardrobe assistant doesn't have its lighter moments or can't be rewarding. If you love clothes, find films and TV fascinating, and enjoy working as part of a team and seeing a project through to fruition, you're likely to be quite happy in the position.

Pitfalls

If you crave recognition and praise, you might be disappointed as a wardrobe assistant. Your job is to back up and support the wardrobe director, who has more direct contact with actors. After you've been in the field for a while and have gained some experience, however, you're likely to assume additional responsibilities and be exposed to more people within the production. Working hours for wardrobe assistants can be long and the work tiring.

Perks

If you love fabrics and fashion and you want to learn more about them, you might think of a position as a wardrobe assistant as on-the-job training. Even if you're just interested in learning more about the entertainment industry, you'll have that opportunity as a wardrobe assistant. You'll have a great chance to meet (or at least peek at) stars, and be involved in the exciting entertainment industry.

Get a Jump on the Job

For starters, try getting a job in a clothing store and begin learning all you can about fabrics and how clothing is constructed. Practice sewing by making your own clothing, or clothing for your friends or family. Look for books on the history of fashion and costuming (see the listing in Read More About It at the back of this book). Get involved with wardrobe in your high school plays and your community "little" theater productions. Lots of small local theaters host classes for kids, or special summer workshops; check these out, especially if there are costuming classes offered.

APPENDIX A: ASSOCIATIONS, ORGANIZATIONS, AND WEB SITES

GENERAL ENTERTAINMENT ORGANIZATIONS

Academy of Motion Picture Arts and Sciences
Academy Foundation
8949 Wilshire Boulevard
Beverly Hills, CA 90211
(310) 247-3000
ampas@oscars.org
http://www.oscars.org/index.html

The Academy of Motion Picture Arts and Sciences, a professional honorary organization of over 6,000 motion picture professionals, was founded to advance the arts and sciences of motion pictures; foster cooperation among creative leaders for cultural, educational, and technological progress; recognize outstanding achievements; cooperate on technical research and improvement of methods and equipment; provide a common forum and meeting ground for various branches and crafts; represent the viewpoint of actual creators of the motion picture; and foster educational activities between the professional community and the public-at-large. The Academy Awards Presentation is also the academy's most important activity and has enabled the organization to maintain a varied year-round calendar of programs and events and a wide-ranging educational and cultural agenda. After more than seven decades of recognizing excellence in filmmaking achievement,
the presentation of the Oscars has become the Academy of Motion Picture Arts and Sciences' most famous activity.

Entertainment Services and Technology Association (ESTA)
875 Sixth Avenue, Suite 1005
New York, NY 10001
(212) 244-1505
info@esta.org
http://www.esta.org

ESTA is a nonprofit trade association representing the entertainment technology industry, with more than 450 members worldwide, in 250 cities, five provinces, and 21 countries. ESTA members represent a wide variety of companies working behind the scenes in the entertainment industry, representing a wide variety of companies specializing in the areas of lighting, scenery, rigging, special effects, sound, costuming, and makeup. Manufacturing members design and manufacture products that are particular to the entertainment industry, such as lighting fixtures, dimming and control, color filters, projected images, rigging materials, atmospheric effects, scenic supplies, audio equipment, and much more. Dealer members specify, distribute, install, and service this equipment for the end user. Affiliate members are the creative teams that envision the production or performance space, and those that are responsible for bringing those visions to life.

**National Academy
of Television Arts and Sciences**
5220 Lankershim Boulevard
North Hollywood, CA 91601-3109
(818) 754-2800
http://www.emmys.org

*The National Academy of Television
Arts and Sciences has more than
12,000 members. Membership in the
academy is open to those persons who
are or who have been actively engaged
in activities related to the production
or distribution of audiovisual works
for national exhibition by means of
telecommunications. The Academy
of Television membership has unique
requirements for each of the 27 peer
groups, described at http://www.emmys.
org/membership/requirements.php.
There are six types of membership in the
academy: Active, Associate, Academic,
Emeritus, Los Angeles Area, and Life
(Honorary). Everyone joins for different
reasons, at different times, for different
career objectives. Members receive
invitations to industry-related academy
events and seminars throughout the year,
as well as a subscription to the award-
winning EMMY magazine.*

**National Association
of Schools of Theater (NAST)**
11250 Roger Bacon Drive, Suite 21
Reston, VA 20190
(703) 437-0700
info@arts-accredit.org
http://nast.arts-accredit.org

*Founded in 1969, NAST is an
organization of schools, conservatories,
colleges, and universities. It has
approximately 135 accredited
institutional members. It establishes
national standards for undergraduate and
graduate degrees and other credentials.
NAST provides information to potential
students and parents, consultations,
statistical information, professional
development, and policy analysis.*

American Film Institute (AFI)
2021 North Western Avenue
Los Angeles, CA 90027-1657
(323) 856-7600
http://www.afi.com

*A national institute providing leadership
in screen education and the recognition
and celebration of excellence in the
art of film, television, and digital
media, AFI trains the next generation
of filmmakers at its conservatory,
maintains films through the AFI Catalog
of Feature Films, and explores new
digital technologies in entertainment
and education through its New Media
Ventures. AFI Awards honors the most
outstanding motion pictures and TV
programs of the year. During the past 32
years, AFI'S Life Achievement Award has
become the highest honor for a career in
film.*

International Animated Film Society
721 South Victory Boulevard
Burbank, CA 91502
(818) 842-8330
info@asifa-hollywood.org
http://www.asifa-hollywood.org

*A worldwide organization dedicated to
the art of animation founded in 1957 in
France, and chartered under UNESCO
in 1960 as a membership organization
devoted to the encouragement and
dissemination of film animation as an art
and communication form. In its 40-year
existence, it has grown to over 1,700
members in 55 countries.*

ENTERTAINMENT GUILDS AND UNIONS

Unions are very important in the entertainment industry. Virtually all film production companies and TV networks sign contracts with union locals that require the employment of workers according to union contracts. Nonunion workers may be hired because of a special talent, to fill a specific need, or for a short period.

Although union membership is not mandated, nonunion workers risk eligibility for future work assignments. There are several different unions representing three different acting fields:

* The Screen Actors Guild (SAG) represents film actors (including television, commercials, and movies).
* Actors' Equity Association (AEA) represents theatrical actors and stage managers.
* The American Federation of Television and Radio Artists (AFTRA) represents members in news and broadcasting; entertainment programming; the recording business; and commercials and nonbroadcast, industrial, and educational media.
* The American Guild of Variety Artists (AGVA) represents certain performers in Broadway, off-Broadway, and cabaret productions, as well as nightclub entertainers and theme park performers.
* The Dramatists Guild of America (DGA) is the professional association of playwrights, composers, and lyricists.
* International Alliance of Theatrical Stage Employees, Moving Picture Technicians, Artists and Allied Crafts (IATSE) represents art directors, cartoonists, editors, costumers, scenic artists, set designers, camera operators, sound technicians, projectionists, and shipping, booking, and other distribution employees.
* Directors Guild of America includes film and TV directors.
* Society of Stage Directors and Choreographers (SSDC) represents choreographers and directors for Broadway, national tours, regional theaters, dinner theaters, and summer stock, as well as choreographers for television, music video, and film.

All these unions have a one-time initiation fee, plus annual dues, which are calculated based on an actor's earnings.

Joining any unions can give you some great benefits, including health care and access to a credit union. But you've also got to realize that once you join, you're no longer allowed to take a nonunion role. That's why beginners usually remain nonunion as long as they can—to gain experience in smaller roles before having to compete with more experienced actors in union-only jobs. All Broadway theaters, major off-Broadway productions, and large regional theaters operate according to Actors' Equity Association rules; to act in these productions, you must be a union member. What's more, if you've been doing lead roles for years in nonunion theater productions, you may be back on the sidelines or in bit parts once again in union shows, because now you'll be competing with top professionals.

All studio produced films, and most independent feature films as well as TV soap operas, series, and movies, require that you be a member of the Screen Actors Guild (SAG). The American Federation of Television and Radio Artists (AFTRA) shares some responsibilities with SAG, but represents a wider range of professionals in many different entertainment categories. SAG is primarily concerned with wages and working conditions of performers working on film.

Actors Equity
165 West 46th Street, 15th Floor
New York, NY 10036
(212) 869-8530

American Federation of Television and Radio Artists (AFTRA)
260 Madison Avenue
New York, NY 10016
(212) 532-0800
http://www.aftra.org/aftra/aftra.htm

A national labor union representing nearly 80,000 performers, journalists, and other artists working in the entertainment and news media. AFTRA's scope of representation covers broadcast, public and cable television (news, sports and weather, drama and comedy, soaps, talk and variety shows, documentaries, children's programming, reality and game shows), radio (news, commercials, hosted programs), sound recordings (CDs, singles, Broadway cast albums, audio books), "non-broadcast" and industrial material, as well as Internet and digital programming.

American Guild of Musical Artists
1430 Broadway, 14th Floor
New York, NY 10018
(212) 265-3687
AGMA@MusicalArtists.org
http://www.musicalartists.org/HomePage.htm

The labor organization that represents opera and concert singers, production

personnel and dancers at principal opera, concert, and dance companies throughout the United States. Soloists and choristers, dancers, choreographers, stage managers, stage directors—they are all part of AGMA

American Guild of Variety Artists
184 5th Avenue, 6th Floor
New York, NY 10010
(212) 675-1003

Association of Theatrical Press Agents and Managers (ATPAM)
1560 Broadway
New York, NY 10036
(212) 719-3666
http://www.atpam.com

ATPAM members are press agents, publicity and marketing specialists, company managers, and house and facilities managers who are devoted to the health, vitality, and success of staged entertainment of all types. ATPAM is part of the International Alliance of Theatrical and Stage Employees, Moving Picture Technicians, Artists and Allied Crafts of the United States, Its Territories and Canada, AFL-CIO, CLC. As Local 18032 of the IATSE, ATPAM enjoys membership in the largest union governing the entertainment business and with that, finds itself part of a vital, growing industry that encompasses stage, screen, and television.

Directors Guild of America (DGA)
7920 Sunset Boulevard
Los Angeles, California 90046
(310) 289-2000
http://www.dga.org

The Directors Guild of America represents more than 12,000 members working in U.S. cities and abroad. Their creative work is represented in theatrical, industrial, educational, and documentary films and television, as well as videos and commercials. Today, through the collective voice of more than 12,700 members that the DGA represents, the guild seeks to protect directorial teams' legal and artistic rights, contend for their creative freedom, and strengthen their ability to develop meaningful and credible careers. The DGA represents Film and Television Directors, Unit Production Managers, First Assistant Directors, Second Assistant Directors, Technical Coordinators and Tape Associate Directors, Stage Managers, and Production Associates.

To join in any guild category, you must obtain employment with a company that has signed a collective bargaining agreement with the guild. While the DGA's Director, Technical Coordinator, and Production Assistant categories don't require members to meet specific criteria before accepting employment, the following categories do:

* *In Film: Unit Production Manager, First Assistant Director, Second Assistant Director*

* *In Tape: Associate Director, Stage Manager*

IATSE Local 161 Script Supervisors
630 Ninth Avenue
New York, NY 10036
(212) 977-9655

IATSE Local 817 Theatrical Teamsters
1 Hollow Lane
Lake Success, NY 11042
(516) 365-3470

IATSE Local 829 United Scenic Artists
16 West 61st Street, 11th Floor

New York, NY 10023
(212) 581-0300

International Brotherhood of Electrical Workers
1125 15th Street, NW
Washington, DC 20005
(202) 833-7000
IBEWnet@compuserve.com
http.//www.ibew.org

The IBEW is a union representing people in a broad range of industries, including the entertainment industry, throughout the United States and Canada.

International Cinematographers Guild
7755 Sunset Boulevard
Hollywood, CA 90046
(323) 876-0160
http://www.cameraguild.com

Guild represents the most talented camera professionals in the world. Guild technicians and artisans are the creators of the visual images on the big screen, the television screen and—as we move into the 21st century—our computer screen. International Cinematographers Guild members—Directors of Photography, Camera Operators and Assistants, Computer Graphics Specialists, Visual Effects Supervisors, Still Photographers and more—are part of the International Alliance of Theatrical Stage Employees. The IATSE is comprised of highly skilled technicians working in film, television, live entertainment, animation, special effects, and new media. To be eligible to work on a production under an IATSE contract, certain requirements must be met regarding industry experience. The specific number of hours, however, may vary according to where you live and work.

Motion Picture Editors Guild
7715 Sunset Boulevard, Suite 200
Hollywood, CA 90046
(800) 705-8700
http://www.editorsguild.com

*The Motion Picture Editors Guild is a
national labor organization currently
representing over 6,000 freelance and
staff postproduction professionals.
Originally formed by Hollywood picture
editors in the 1930s who were seeking
a voice on the job and decent working
conditions, the guild has grown into an
open, forward-thinking organization
that embraces new technology and,
above all, endeavors to protect and
improve the interests of guild members.
As Local 700 of the International
Alliance of Theatrical Stage Employees
(IATSE), an international union more
than 100 years old, they are allied with
some 500 affiliated locals in the United
States and Canada with a combined
membership of more than 104,000. This
strength increases collective power at
the bargaining table and results in better
contracts with superior benefits.*

*The guild's goal is to continue to
organize non-represented professionals
in every aspect of postproduction.
This means not only feature films and
traditional network television, but
also reality TV, cable programming,
documentaries, music videos,
commercials, and industrials. Indeed,
there is no area of visual media
postproduction the guild is not interested
in organizing, including the Internet and
video gaming.*

*With regional offices in Hollywood,
New York City, and Chicago, the Motion
Picture Editors Guild is committed to
the aid and protection of its members,
so they are better able to focus on their
careers and advance their craft to the
highest possible levels.*

Musicians Union Local 802
322 West 48th Street
New York, NY 10036
(212) 245-4802
http://www.local802afm.org

National Writers Union
113 University Place, 6th Floor
New York, NY 10003
(212) 254-0279
nwu@nwu.org
http://www.nwu.org

*The only labor union that represents
freelance writers in all genres, formats,
and media, the NWU offers its members
grievance assistance, contract advice,
a job hotline, health and professional
liability insurance, and much more. With
the combined strength of 3,500 members
in 17 local chapters nationwide, and with
the support of the United Automobile
Workers (UAW), the NWU works to
advance the economic and working
conditions of writers. They do this by
challenging the corporate media giants,
lobbying Congress to pass legislation that
protects the rights of writers, creating
viable solutions to provide publishers fair
alternatives to unfair practices, and by
educating and empowering members.*

Screen Actors Guild (SAG)
5757 Wilshire Boulevard
Los Angeles, CA 90036-3600
(800) SAG-0767
and
360 Madison Avenue 12th Floor
New York, NY 10017
(212) 944-1030
http://www.sag.org

*Screen Actors Guild is the nation's
premier labor union representing actors.
Established in 1933, SAG has a rich
history in the American labor movement,
from standing up to studios to break
long-term engagement contracts in*

the 1940s to fighting for artists' rights amid the digital revolution of the 21st century. With 20 branches nationwide, SAG represents nearly 120,000 actors in film, television, industrials, commercials, and music videos. The guild exists to enhance actors' working conditions, compensation and benefits, and to be a powerful, unified voice on behalf of artists' rights. SAG is a proud affiliate of the AFL-CIO.

Writers Guild of America (WGA)—WGA West
7000 West Third Street
Los Angeles, CA 90048
(800) 548-4532)
http://www.wga.org

Writers Guild of America (WGA)—WGA East
555 West 57th Street
New York, NY 10019
(212) 767-7800
http://www.wgaeast.org

The WGA is a labor union that represents more than 8,500 professional writers who create your favorite films and television programs. The WGA traditionally is involved with contract negotiations with producers and studios on behalf of all writers.

ANIMAL WRANGLER

The Delta Society
875 124th Avenue NE, Suite 101
Bellevue, WA 98005
(425) 226-7357
http://www.deltasociety.org
info@deltasociety.org

The Delta Society is a coalition of animal trainers, humane societies, and animal welfare centers that works to promote the rights of animals and to teach more

effective and humane training methods. The Delta Society in 2001 compiled and published a book called, Professional Standards for Dog Trainers: Effective, Humane Principles. Veterinarians, certified animal behaviorists, professional animal trainers, and others contributed to the comprehensive book. The Delta Society offers training workshops and informational materials, and matches appropriate pets to owners.

BEST BOY

Independent Electrical Contractors, Inc. (IEC)
4401 Ford Avenue, Suite 1100
Alexandria, VA 22302
(703) 549-7558
info@ieci.org
http://www.ieci.org

IEC is a trade association for independent electrical contractors. For almost 50 years, IEC has represented the needs of electrical contractors, offering trade shows, educational opportunities, governmental affairs representation, and an annual convention. Based in Alexandria, Virginia, the association has more than 75 chapters nationwide.

BOOM OPERATOR

Cinema Audio Society
12414 Huston Street
Valley Village, CA 91607
(818) 752-8624
CASOffice@cinemaaudiosociety.org
http://www.cinemaaudiosociety.org

The Cinema Audio Society was founded in 1964 as a means of allowing sound mixers to share information. There are three levels of membership. Full *membership is open to production and postproduction sound mixers who work on feature films, television, commercials, and music scoring. Associate membership is open to sound editors, technicians, microphone boom operators, and recordists. Corporate membership is open to companies that specialize in audio and video. The society sponsors numerous educational opportunities for sound mixers and others, and holds an annual awards banquet to recognize outstanding contribution to the field. A not-for-profit organization, the Cinema Audio Society also publishes the* Journal of the Cinema Audio Society.

CAMERA OPERATORS

Association of Independent Video & Filmmakers (AIVF)
304 Hudson Street, 6th Floor
New York, NY 10013
(212) 807-1400
info@aivf.org
http://www.aivf.org

A 30-year-old national trade association based in New York City, providing support to individual media artists and producers. Established by a group of independent filmmakers, AIVF is the largest national organization representing independent media artists working at all levels across all genres. AIVF members number over 5,000 individuals (from students to Academy Award winners) and 350 businesses across the country. The organization tries to increase the creative and professional opportunities for independent video and filmmakers and to enhance the growth of independent media by providing services, advocacy,

and information. The organization also attempts to create new opportunities for the field; to engender a strong sense of community among the very diverse constituencies of independent media artists; and to promote media arts to a broader public.

Society of Operating Cameramen (SOC)
PO Box 2006
Toluca Lake, CA 91610
(818) 382-7070
http://www.soc.org

An honorary organization composed of several hundred men and women who make their living operating film and/or video cameras in the cinematic media and have been recognized for their work. The SOC recognizes and promotes excellence in camera operation and in the allied camera crafts, and encourages development of both technology and production methods that will aid and assist members. It also publishes a semi-annual magazine called The Operating Cameraman. *Qualified camera operators are given active membership. Camera assistants, directors of photography, and still photographers carry associate membership status. Corporate affiliate memberships are also available.*

Steadicam Operators Association
5 Waterford Court
Monroe Township, NJ 08831
info@steadicam-ops.com
http://www.steadicam-ops.com

Formed by Garrett Brown, the inventor of the Steadicam, and Nicola Pecorini in 1988 to connect skilled Steadicam operators with motion picture directors and producers. Today, the Steadicam Operators Association represents Steadicam operators around the world, providing referrals across the entire film and video industry. Additional services include organizing and conducting Steadicam workshops.

CASTING DIRECTOR

Casting Society of America (CSA)
145 W. 28th Street, 12th floor
New York, NY 10001
(212) 868-1260
info@castingsociety.com
http://www.castingsociety.com

The Casting Society of America is the largest organization worldwide representing casting directors. With more than 350 members, CSA represents casting directors in the United States, England, Australia, Italy, and Canada. The association works to provide an industry standard for casting, to represent the interests of its members, and provide opportunity for communication among members. Founded in 1982, it was originally known as The American Society of Casting Directors. The name was changed in 1984 to the Casting Society of America. The society presents Artios Awards each year for outstanding achievement in casting.

CELEBRITY ASSISTANT

Association of Celebrity Personal Assistants
914 Westwood Boulevard PMB 507
Los Angeles, CA 90024
(310) 281-7755
http://www.celebrityassistants.org

The Association of Celebrity Personal Assistants was founded in Los Angeles in 1992 in order to provide support for celebrity assistants in the form of networking opportunities and to promote public awareness about celebrity assistants. The organization holds monthly membership meetings with professional development and networking opportunities. It also publishes a bi-monthly newsletter called The Right Hand; *provides members with access to industry statistics such as wages, average job duration, and so forth; and features an online job bank and membership directory. The organization's Web site contains tips for people wishing to become celebrity assistants.*

New York Celebrity Assistants
459 Columbus Avenue #216
New York, NY 10024
(212) 803-5444
http://www.nycelebrityassistants.org

With a mission to promote the professional standing of celebrity assistants, New York Celebrity Assistants was founded in 1994 in New York City. The organization holds monthly meetings that include programs geared toward professional development, entertainment, and networking opportunities. A yearly "best of the best" meeting at which celebrity assistants share tips and information has resulted in a book called The Best of The Best. *The book is available to members, along with job referral services and other perks. Membership to the organization is limited to celebrity assistants who have worked for at least one year. Its Web site contains tips for people wishing to become celebrity assistants.*

CELEBRITY PHOTOGRAPHER

**Professional Photographers
of America, Inc. (PPA)**
229 Peachtree Street NE, Suite 2200
Atlanta, GA 30303
(404) 522-8600
http://www.ppa.com

The Professional Photographers of America, Inc. is the largest organization of professional photographers in the world, boasting more than 14,000 members in 64 countries. Founded in 1880 as a source of education and community for photographers, the organization currently offers business and personal insurance for its members, business discounts, professional recognition, credential programs, and advocacy services. Members also receive a twice-monthly e-mailed newsletter.

CLOWN

World Clown Association
PO Box 77236
Corona, CA 92877-0107
(800) 336-7922
http://www.worldclownassociation.com

The purpose of the World Clown Association is to promote the art of clowning and educate people about clown arts. It was founded in 1983. Eight members of the World Clown Association have been inducted into the International Clown Hall of Fame. The organization is divided into 10 regions, including a Canadian region, Latin American region and an overseas region. The association has online directories of member clowns, special sites for kids, and an online store for clown supplies and other items. It also sponsors a yearly convention, at which the association names a clown of the year.

Clowns of America International (COAI)
PO Box C
Richeyville, PA 15358-0532
(888) 552-CLOWN
ASKUS@coai.org
http://www.clownsofamerica.org

Clowns of America International is an organization with a goal of helping professional and amateur clowns achieve success, and to provide opportunities for education, support, networking, and job sharing. The organization publishes The New Calliope, a magazine that is mailed to members every other month. Clowns of America International holds a yearly, international convention, which includes competitions, workshops, and educational programs. Anyone interested in clowning, including children, may join the organization.

COMEDIAN

Comedy Zone
http://www.comedy-zone.net/zones/standup.htm

Web site begun in 1999 that includes thousands of pages of original content plus a comprehensive directory of the best humor-related Web sites, along with comedy information, quotations, cartoons, and much more.

DIRECTOR OF PHOTOGRAPHY

**Association of Independent Video
& Filmmakers (AIVF)**

304 Hudson Street, 6th Floor
New York, NY 10013
(212) 807-1400
info@aivf.org
http://www.aivf.org

A 30-year old national trade association based in New York City, providing support to individual media artists and producers. Established by a group of independent filmmakers, AIVF is the largest national organization representing independent media artists working at all levels across all genres. AIVF members number more than 5,000 individuals (from students to Academy Award winners) and 350 businesses across the country. The organization tries to increase the creative and professional opportunities for independent video and filmmakers and to enhance the growth of independent media by providing services, advocacy, and information. The organization also attempts to create new opportunities for the field; to engender a strong sense of community among the very diverse constituencies of independent media artists; and to promote media arts to a broader public.

Society of Operating Cameramen (SOC)
PO Box 2006
Toluca Lake, CA 91610
(818) 382-7070 (24-hour message)
http://www.soc.org

An honorary organization composed of several hundred men and women who make their living operating film and/or video cameras in the cinematic media and have been recognized for their work. The SOC recognizes and promotes excellence in camera operation and in the allied camera crafts, and encourages development of both technology and production methods that will aid and assist members. It also publishes a semi-

annual magazine called The Operating Cameraman. *Qualified camera operators are given active membership. Camera assistants, directors of photography, and still photographers carry associate membership status. Corporate affiliate memberships are also available*

Steadicam Operators Association
5 Waterford Court
Monroe Township, NJ 08831
info@steadicam-ops.com
http://www.steadicam-ops.com

Formed by Garrett Brown, the inventor of the Steadicam, and Nicola Pecorini in 1988 to connect skilled Steadicam operators with motion picture directors and producers. Today, the Steadicam Operators Association represents Steadicam operators around the world, providing referrals across the entire film and video industry. Additional services include organizing and conducting Steadicam workshops.

DOCUMENTARY FILMMAKER

American Cinema Editors (ACE)
1041 North Formosa Avenue
West Hollywood, CA 90046
(323) 850-2900
http://www.ace-filmeditors.org

An honorary organization of distinguished film editors who are dedicated to the understanding, appreciation, and advancement of motion picture editing.

Association of Independent Video & Filmmakers (AIVF)
304 Hudson Street, 6th Floor
New York, NY 10013
(212) 807-1400
info@aivf.org

http://www.aivf.org

A 30-year old national trade association based in New York City, providing support to individual media artists and producers. Established by a group of independent filmmakers, AIVF is the largest national organization representing independent media artists working at all levels across all genres. AIVF members number over 5,000 individuals (from students to Academy Award winners) and 350 businesses across the country. The organization tries to increase the creative and professional opportunities for independent video and filmmakers and to enhance the growth of independent media by providing services, advocacy, and information. The organization also attempts to create new opportunities for the field; to engender a strong sense of community among the very diverse constituencies of independent media artists; and to promote media arts to a broader public.

International Documentary Association (IDA)
1201 West 5th Street, Suite M320
Los Angeles, CA 90017
(213) 534-3600
info@documentary.org
http://www.documentary.org

The mission of the International Documentary Association is to promote nonfiction film and video around the world by recognizing the efforts of documentary film and video makers, increasing public appreciation and demand for the documentary, and providing a forum for documentary makers, their supporters and suppliers.

Studentfilmmakers.com
1123 Broadway, #902

New York, NY 10010
http://www.studentfilmmakers.com

An online community for video and film making, offering workshops, internships, classified ads, news, a magazine, and much more.

FIGHT CHOREOGRAPHER

Society of American Fight Directors (SAFD)
587 Lisbon Street
San Francisco, CA 94112
(415) 957-3622
PWRegRep@safd.org
http://www.safd.org/index.html

Organization for fight directors whose purpose is to bring together into one organization those individuals who earn a living choreographing fight scenes for stage and film.

FOCUS PULLER

Society of Operating Cameramen (SOC)
PO Box 2006
Toluca Lake, CA 91610
(818) 382-7070
http://www.soc.org

An honorary organization composed of several hundred men and women who make their living operating film and/or video cameras in the cinematic media and have been recognized for their work. The SOC recognizes and promotes excellence in camera operation and in the allied camera crafts, and encourages development of both technology and production methods that will aid and assist members. It also publishes a semi-annual magazine called The Operating

Cameraman. *Qualified camera operators are given active membership. Camera assistants, directors of photography, and still photographers carry associate membership status. Corporate affiliate memberships are also available*

LOCATION SCOUT

Location Works
42 Old Compton Street
London, W1D 4TX, UK
+44 (0) 20 7494 0888
info@locationworks.com
http://www.locationworks.com

Location Works is a team of experienced location scouts that have worked all over the world. Its Web site offers career advice, links to other sites, a location library, portfolio, descriptions of shoots, information about being a location scout, and a mailing feature so you can send any questions you might have.

MOTIVATIONAL SPEAKER

The National Speakers Association (NSA)
1500 S. Priest Drive
Tempe, AZ 85281
(480) 968-2552
http://www.nsaspeaker.org

Founded in 1973, the NSA is the largest international organization for professional speakers. The association has grown from 80 members to more than 2,000, with 37 state and regional chapters. It sponsors regional workshops and yearly national conferences, and publishes the Professional Speaker *magazine,* Who's Who in Professional

Speaking: The Meeting Planner's Guide, *and the* Voices Of Experience *audio magazine. NSA members who meet certain criteria are designated as certified speaking professionals.*

American Speakers Bureau Corporation
10151 University Boulevard, #197
Orlando, FL 32817
(407) 826-4248
info@speakersbureau.com
http://www.speakersbureau.com

The ASBC is an organization that matches speakers with events nationwide. Founded in 1989, the ASBC screens and selects speakers to be its members, and then refers speakers to clients depending on subject matter, availability, location, and other factors.

OPERA SINGER

Center for Contemporary Opera
PO Box 258
New York, NY 10044-0205
(212) 758-2757
http://www.conopera.org

Organization dedicated to the creation and performance of contemporary American opera and opera in English; sponsors International Opera Singers Competition with no age limit. The organization hopes to assist American composers and composers writing in English by producing their opera/musical theater works on the professional stage; to assist the most talented singers worldwide with their operatic careers, and to inform the general public about contemporary opera through lectures, panels, previews, and through its publication Opera Today.

Opera America
1156 15th Street NW, Suite 810
Washington, DC 20005
(202) 293-4466
frontdesk@operaamerica.org
http://www.operaam.org

*Organization that provides a variety
of informational, technical, and
administrative resources to the greater
opera community; its fundamental
mission is to promote opera as exciting
and accessible to individuals from all
walks of life; membership includes 169
company members around the world,
plus affiliate and business members, and
individual members from 48 states, seven
Canadian provinces, and 19 countries
abroad, representing Australia, Asia,
Europe, Africa, North America, and
South America.*

**National Association of Teachers of
Singing (NATS)**
4745 Sutton Park Court, Suite #201
Jacksonville FL 32224
(904) 992-9101
info@nats.org
http://www.nats.org

*Alleged to be the largest association of
teachers of singing in the world with over
5,000 members; encourages the highest
standards of singing through excellence
in teaching and the promotion of vocal
education and research.*

ORCHESTRA CONDUCTOR

The American Symphony League
33 West 60th Street, Fifth Floor
New York, NY 10023
(212) 262-5161
info@symphony.org
http://www.symphony.org

*The American Symphony League
seeks to assist orchestras and promote
orchestral music to the public. With
about 1,000 members from symphony,
youth, chamber, and collegiate
orchestras, the league offers information
about workshops, seminars, and classes
held at locations all across the country.
Its Web site provides a career board
that allows conductors to submit their
resumes to be reviewed by member
orchestras that have current job
openings. The American Symphony
League was founded in 1942 and was
chartered by Congress in 1962.*

The Conductors Guild
PO Box 18398
Richmond, VA 23226
(804) 553-1378
http://www.conductorsguild.org

*The Conductors Guild is devoted
exclusively to serving orchestra
conductors and promoting the art of
conducting. It was founded in 1975 as
an offshoot of the American Symphony
Orchestra League. In 1985 it became
an independent organization, and
has grown to include nearly 2,000
individual, institutional, and library
members. The Conductors Guild is a
member of the National Music Council
and has members from all 50 states
and more than 40 other countries. The
guild publishes a semi-annual journal,
a quarterly newsletter, an annual
membership directory, and a monthly
job bulletin for conductors. Membership
is open to conductors and institutions
affiliated with instrumental and/or vocal
music in areas including symphony and
chamber orchestras, opera, chorus, music
theater, wind ensemble, ballet and other
forms of dance, and band.*

PRODUCT PLACEMENT SPECIALIST

Entertainment Resources and Marketing Association (ERMA)
1045 East Road
La Habra Heights, CA 90631
http://www.erma.org

Association of professionals working in entertainment marketing and brand integration. ERMA is comprised of product placement agencies, corporations, production companies, and studios. ERMA's active members include many Fortune 500 companies and their agencies representing America's most beloved and best-known products. These brands often become co-stars in the film or television show in which they appear and benefit additionally by exposure to millions of consumers in international markets. These entertainment properties offer unique promotional opportunities for themed promotions, publicity, advertising, and point of sale merchandising.

PROP MASTER

The Society of Prop Artisan Managers (SPAM)
140 West Washington Street
Indianpolis, IN 46204
http://www.geocities.com/
Broadway/2938/home.html

The Society of Prop Artisan Managers is a group devoted to providing information and educational opportunities for people working as prop masters or interested in entering the career field. Membership is limited to those who are employed as prop masters at a theater with

membership in the League of Resident Theaters.

PUPPETEER

The Center for Puppetry Arts
1404 Spring Street NW at 18th
Atlanta, GA 30309-2820
(404) 873-3089
http://www.puppet.org

The Center for Puppetry Arts is a unique, nonprofit organization that offers puppet workshops and classes for children and adults, distance learning opportunities, a puppet museum, a puppet store, a theater in which puppet performances are staged, and much more. The 25-year-old organization is a member of the Atlanta Coalition of Performing Arts and is the U.S. headquarters of the Union International de la Marionnette, an international puppet association that claims to be the oldest theater-related group in the world. The Center for Puppetry Arts opened on September 23, 1978, when the famous late puppeteer, Jim Henson, and his famous frog puppet, Kermit, cut the center's ceremonial ribbon.

The Jim Henson Foundation
627 Broadway, 9th floor
New York, NY 10012
(212) 680-1400
info@hensonfoundation.org
http://www.hensonfoundation.org

The Henson Foundation offers grants to puppeteers or organizations that promote the art of puppetry in the United States. Founded in 1982 by Jim Henson, the creator of the famous Muppets, the foundation has awarded more than 350 grants to puppeteers, puppet creators, and puppetry organizations. From 1992 until 2000, the foundation sponsored a biannual international festival in order to expose people around the world to the art of puppetry. The Henson Foundation maintains an extensive video collection of regional, national, and international puppet performances, and publishes a biweekly newsletter called Puppet Happenings.

Puppeteers of America
PO Box 330
West Liberty, IA 52776
(888) 568-6235
http://www.puppeteers.org

Founded in 1937, the Puppeteers of America is a national, nonprofit organization dedicated to promoting the art of puppetry, encouraging puppet performances, and creating community among puppeteers. It sponsors a yearly National Day of Puppetry, a national festival, and regional festivals. Members can use the organization to search for jobs in the field of puppetry, buy and sell puppets, and meet other puppeteers. Membership in Puppeteers of America is open to anyone with a love of and interest in puppetry.

Rick Lyon and the Lyon Puppets
http://lyonpuppets.com

The Web site of Rick Lyon, a professional puppeteer in New York City. You can find information about building puppets, becoming a puppeteer, and the art of puppetry.

SCENE CONSTRUCTION EXPERT

Association of Theatrical Artists and Craftspeople

604 Riverside Drive
New York, NY 10031
(212) 234-9001

Publishers of the Entertainment Sourcebook, which provides information on theatrical artists and craftspeople.

SCREENWRITER

American Screenwriters Association (ASA)
269 South Beverly Drive, Suite 2600
Beverly Hills, CA 90212-3807
(866) 265-9091
asa@goasa.com
http://www.asascreenwriters.com

Nonprofit group organized for educational purposes, including the promotion and encouragement of the art of screenwriting. ASA is committed to the international support and advancement of all screenwriters, and welcomes interested individuals from around the world who are pursuing the writing of documentaries, educational films, feature films, television, and even radio and large screen format (Omnimax, IMAX) films. The American Screenwriters Association has an international membership of more than 1,300 members located throughout the United States, Europe, the Pacific and the Middle East in 32 countries and 939 cities.

SET MEDIC

National Association of Emergency Medical Technicians (NAEMT)
PO Box 1400
Clinton, MS 39060
(800) 34-NAEMT
http://www.naemt.org

The oldest and largest national EMS trade association representing all EMTs and paramedics.

SOUND MIXER

Cinema Audio Society (CAS)
12414 Huston Street
Valley Village, CA 91607
(818) 752-8624
CASOffice@cinemaaudiosociety.org
http://www.cinemaaudiosociety.org

The Cinema Audio Society was founded in 1964 as a means of allowing sound mixers to share information. There are three levels of membership. Full membership is open to production and postproduction sound mixers who work on feature films, television, commercials, and music scoring. Associate membership is open to sound editors, technicians, microphone boom operators, and recordists. Corporate membership is open to companies that specialize in audio and video. The society sponsors numerous educational opportunities for sound mixers and others, and holds an annual awards banquet to recognize outstanding contribution to the field. A not-for-profit organization, the Cinema Audio Society also publishes the Journal of the Cinema Audio Society.

Professional Sound
Norris-Whitney Communications
PO Box 670
240 Portage Road, #3
Lewiston, NY 14092
http://www.professional-sound.com

A bimonthly magazine that includes news of interest to sound mixers, classified ads for employment opportunities and equipment sales, and a "Sound Advice"

column that addresses problems of people working in the field of sound.

STORYBOARD ARTIST

International Animated Film Society
721 S. Victory Boulevard
Burbank, CA 91502
(818) 842-8330
info@asifa-hollywood.org
http://www.asifa-hollywood.org

A worldwide organization dedicated to the art of animation founded in 1957 in France, and chartered under UNESCO in 1960 as a membership organization devoted to the encouragement and dissemination of film animation as an art and communication form. In its 40 year existence, it has grown to more than 1,700 members in 55 countries.

National Cartoonists Society
1133 West Morse Boulevard, Suite 201
Winter Park, FL 32789
(407) 647-8839
crowsegal@crowsegal.com
http://www.reuben.org

The world's largest and most prestigious organization of professional cartoonists.

Storyboard Artist Bill Lyle
http://www.billylyle.com/flash.html

The Web site of storyboard artist Bill Lyle, as featured on pages 99–100.

STUDIO TEACHER

On Location Education
http://www.onlocationeducation.com/%5CDefault.aspx?tabid=71

Organization that provides information for people interested in being a studio teacher, and a complete range of services to children in all segments of the entertainment and athletics industries.

Studio Teachers Certification Database
http://www.dir.ca.gov/databases/dlselr/StudTch.html
The database contains the following teacher's information: certificate number; expiration date; name; city; state; and date of data.

STUNT PERFORMER

**Stuntmen's Association
of Motion Pictures**
10660 Riverside Drive, 2nd Floor, Suite E
Toluca Lake, CA 91602
(818) 766-4334
info@stuntmen.com
http://www.stuntmen.com

The Stuntmen's Association of Motion Pictures was founded in 1961 by a group of Hollywood stuntmen who were concerned about the future direction of the stunt business. They observed that the stuntmen weren't perceived as professionals and felt they didn't get the respect that they earned. As an organization, the Stuntmen's Association established high standards for professionalism and expertise, and invited only the best stuntmen to join. Membership is by invitation only, and all members are required to belong to the Screen Actors Guild. The Stuntmen's Association has about 125 members, all of whom are dedicated to performing the highest-quality level of stunts with the maximum degree of safety.

Manny Siverio.com
http://www.mannysiverio.com

The Web site of Manny Siverio, a professional stunt performer and coordinator from New York City. You'll find tips on getting started in stunt work, and lots of information about different types of stunts, the background of stunt work, and more.

VENTRILOQUIST

International Ventriloquists Association
(702) 258-1556
inquista@hotmail.com
http://www.inquista.com

Membership includes a subscription to Distant Voices, a 60-plus page magazine featuring ventriloquist events throughout the world.

Canadian Ventriloquism Association
http://www.ventriloquism.ca
Dedicated to the art of ventriloquism from a Canadian perspective.

Vent Haven ConVENTion
http://www.venthaven.com

The Web site for the Vent Haven ConVENTion, the world's oldest and largest continuing gathering of ventriloquists, held in Fort Mitchell, Kentucky each year.

VOICE-OVER ARTIST

The International Visual Communication Association (IVCA)
http://www.ivca.org
Organization that exists to promote effective business and public service communications of the highest ethical and professional standards. The

association aims to be a center of excellence for best communication practice and works with production companies, freelancers, support service providers, and clients of the industry to represent their interests and help maximize their competitiveness and professionalism.

WARDROBE ASSISTANT

Costume Society of America
PO Box 73
Earleville, MD 21929
(800) CSA-9447
http://www.costumesocietyamerica.com

The Costume Society of America seeks to promote the study of dress and costume, and to raise the professionalism and credibility of people who work with wardrobe. The society is divided into regions and sponsors regional meetings and events. Members are encouraged to network amongst themselves and with members of other groups that share their interests in costume and wardrobe.

APPENDIX B:
ONLINE CAREER RESOURCES

This volume offers a look inside a wide range of unusual and unique careers that might appeal to someone interested in entertainment. While this book highlights general information about each job, it's really only a glimpse into these unusual careers. The entries are intended to merely whet your appetite, and provide you with some career options you maybe never knew existed.

Before jumping into any career, you'll want to do more research to make sure that it's really something you want to pursue. This way, as you continue to do research and talk to experts in particular fields, you can ask informed and intelligent questions that will help you make your decisions. To do this, you'll need to be able to locate those people. You might want to research the education options for learning the skills you'll need to be successful, along with scholarships, work-study programs, and other opportunities to help you finance that education. And you might want answers to questions that were not addressed in the information provided here. If you search long enough, you can find just about anything on the Internet, including additional information about the jobs featured in this book.

✴ **A word about Internet safety:** The Internet is a wonderful resource for networking. Many job and career sites have forums where students can interact with others working in those fields. Some sites offer online chat rooms where visitors can interact with each other. This provides students and jobseekers opportunities to make connections and begin to establish some contacts to help with future employment.

These days, most students learn about Internet safety in school computer classes. But we want to emphasize safety issues here: As you visit these forums and chat rooms, remember that anyone could be on the other side of that computer screen telling you exactly what you want to hear. It's easy to get wrapped up in the excitement of the moment when you're in a forum or a chat, interacting with people who share your career dreams. Be cautious about what kind of personal information you make available on the forums and in the chats; never give out your full name, address, or phone number. And never agree to meet with someone you've met online.

SEARCH ENGINES

When looking for information, there are many search engines you could use besides the well-known Google to help you find out more about adventurous jobs. You may already have a favorite search engine, but you might want to take some time to check out some of the others. Some have features that might help you find information you couldn't locate anywhere else. Several engines offer suggestions for ways to narrow your results, or suggest related phrases you might want to use. This is handy if you are having trouble locating exactly what you want.

It's also a good idea to learn how to use the advanced search features of your favorite search engines. Knowing the advanced possibilities might help you to zero in on exactly the information for which you're searching without wasting time looking through pages of irrelevant hits.

As you use the Internet to search information on the perfect career, keep in mind that like anything you find on the Internet, you need to consider the source from which the information comes.

Some of the most popular Internet search engines are:

AllSearchEngines.com
http://www.allsearchengines.com

This search engine index has links to the major search engines along with search engines grouped by topic. The site includes a page with more than 75 career and job search engines at http://www.allsearchengines.com/careerjobs.html.

AlltheWeb
http://www.alltheweb.com

AltaVista
http://www.altavista.com

Ask.com
http://www.ask.com

Dogpile
http://www.dogpile.com

Excite
http://www.excite.com

Google
http://www.google.com

HotBot
http://www.hotbot.com

LookSmart
http://www.looksmart.com

Lycos
http://www.lycos.com

Mamma.com
http://www.mamma.com

MSN Network
http://www.msn.com

My Way
http://www.goto.com

Teoma
http://www.directhit.com

Vivisimo
http://www.vivisimo.com

Yahoo!
http://www.yahoo.com

HELPFUL WEB SITES

The Internet has a wealth of information on careers—everything from the mundane to the outrageous. There are thousands of sites devoted to helping you find the perfect job for you and your interests, skills, and talents. The sites listed here are some of the most helpful ones the authors discovered while researching the jobs in this volume. These sites, which are listed in alphabetical order, are offered for your information. The authors do not endorse any of the information found on these sites.

All Experts
http://www.allexperts.com

The oldest and largest free Q&A service on the Internet, AllExperts.com has thousands of volunteer experts who can answer your questions on just about anything. You also can read replies to questions asked by other people. Each expert has an online profile to help you pick someone you think might be best suited to answer your question. Very easy to use, it's a great resource for finding experts who can help to answer your questions.

America's Career InfoNet
http://www.acinet.org

This site has a wealth of information! You can get a feel for the general job market; check out wages and trends in a particular state for different jobs; and learn more about the knowledge, skills, abilities, and tasks for specific careers. There is also information about required certifications and how to get them. In addition, you can search for more than 5,000 scholarships and financial opportunities to help pay for your education. This site also maintains a huge career resources library with links to nearly 6,500 online resources. For fun, you can take a break and watch one of nearly 450 videos featuring real people at work—everything from able seamen to zoologists!

Backdoor Jobs: Short-Term Job Adventures, Summer Jobs, Volunteer Vacations, Work Abroad and More
http://www.backdoorjobs.com

This is the Web site of the popular book by the same name, now in its third edition. While not as extensive as the book, the site still offers a wealth of information for people looking for short-term opportunities: internships, seasonal jobs, volunteer vacations, and work abroad. Job opportunities are classified into several categories: Adventure Jobs, Camps, Ranches & Resort Jobs, Ski Resort Jobs, Jobs in the Great Outdoors, Nature Lover Jobs, Sustainable Living and Farming Work, Artistic & Learning Adventures, Heart Work, and Opportunities Abroad.

Career Guide to Industries
http://www.bls.gov/oco/cg/cgindex.htm

For someone interested in working in a specific industry, but who may be undecided about exactly what career to pursue, this site is the place to start. Put together by the U.S. Department of Labor, you can learn more about the industry, working conditions, employment, occupations (in the industry), training and advancement, earnings, outlook, and sources of additional information.

Career Planning at About.com
http://careerplanning.about.com

Just like most of the other About.com topics, the career planning area has a wealth of information, together with links to other information on the Web. Among the essentials are career planning A-to-Z, a career planning glossary, information on career choices, and a free career planning class.

Career Prospects in Virginia
http://www3.ccps.virginia.edu/career_prospects/default-search.html

Career Prospects is a database of entries with information about more than 400 careers. Developed by the Virginia Career Resource Network, the online career information resource of the Virginia Department of Education,

Office of Career and Technical Education Services, was intended as a source of information about jobs important to Virginia—but it's actually a great source of information for anyone. While some of the information (such as wages, outlook, and requirements) may apply only to Virginia, most details—such as what the job's like, getting ahead, skills, and links—will help anyone interested in that career.

Career Voyages
http://www.careervoyages.gov

This "ultimate road trip to career success" is sponsored by the U.S. Department of Labor and the U.S. Department of Education. The site provides specific information in separate sections for students, parents, care changers, and career advisors offers great information started, the high- to find your sure

L.
bro
whic

Fine Livi
http://www
archive/0,16
html#Series87

*The show Radica
Living network loo*

to take a chance and follow their dreams and passions. The show focuses on individuals between the ages of 20 and 65 who have made the decision to leave successful, lucrative careers to start over, usually in an unconventional career. You can read all about these people and their journeys on the show's Web site.

Free Salary Survey Reports and Cost of Living Reports
http://www.salaryexpert.com

Based on information from a number of sources, Salary Expert will tell you what kind of salary you can expect to make for a certain job in a certain geographic location. Salary Expert has information on hundreds of jobs—everything from ore traditional jobs to some unique, f-the-ordinary professions such essurist, blacksmith, denture , taxidermist, and many others. ch sections covering schools, crime, community comparison, and community explorer, this Web site is filled with helpful info. You might also find the "moving center" a useful site for those who need to relocate for training or mployment.

un Jobs
ttp://www.funjobs.com

un Jobs has job listings for adventure, tdoor, and fun jobs at ranches, mps, and ski resorts. The job postings ve a lot of information about the sition, requirements, benefits, and ponsibilities so that you know what are getting into ahead of time. d you can apply online for most of positions. In addition, the "Fun npanies" link will let you look companies in an A-to-Z listing, ou can search for companies in a specific area or by keyword. The company listings offer you more detailed information about the location, types of jobs available, employment qualifications, and more.

Girls Can Do

http://www.girlscando.com

"Helping girls discover their life's passions," this Web site has opportunities, resources, and lots of other cool stuff for girls ages 8 to 18. Visitors can explore sections on Outdoor Adventure, Sports, My Body, The Arts, Sci-Tech, Change the World, and Learn, Earn, and Intern. In addition to reading about women in all sorts of careers, girls can explore a wide range of opportunities and information that will help them grow into strong, intelligent, capable women.

Hot Jobs—Career Tools Home

http://www.hotjobs.com/htdocs/tools/ index-us.html

While the jobs listed at Hot Jobs are more on the traditional side, the Career Tools area has a lot of great resources for anyone looking for a job. You'll find information about how to write a resume and a cover letter, how to put together a career portfolio, interviewing tips, links to career assessments, and much more.

Job Descriptions & Job Details

http://www.job-descriptions.org

Search for descriptions and details for more than 13,000 jobs at this site. You can search for jobs by category or by industry. You'd probably be hard pressed to find a job that isn't listed here, and you'll probably find lots of jobs you never imagined existed. The descriptions and details are short, but it's interesting

and fun, and might lead you to the career of your dreams.

Job Hunter's Bible

http://www.jobhuntersbible.com

This site is the official online supplement to the book What Color Is Your Parachute? A Practical Manual for Job-Hunters and Career-Changers, *and is a great source of information with lots of informative, helpful articles and links to many more resources.*

JobMonkey

http://www.jobmonkey.com

JobMonkey claims to be your gateway to "The Coolest Jobs on Earth," and that they are. Not only can you read all about some of the coolest, most exciting and adventurous jobs in the world, you can search the listings for a really cool job. JobMonkey has listings for summer jobs, seasonal jobs, and full-time jobs around the country and around the world. The Job Hunting Tools section offers valuable advice to help you land the job of your dreams; of special interest is the Travel Center. Caution: Most of the jobs at JobMonkey require you to travel.

Job Profiles

http://www.jobprofiles.org

This site offers a collection of profiles in which experienced workers share rewards of their job, stressful parts of the job, basic skills needed and challenges of the future, together with advice on entering the field. The careers include everything from baseball ticket manager to pastry chef and much, much more. The hundreds of profiles are arranged by broad category, but while most of the profiles are easy to read, you can check out the How to Browse JobProfiles.org section (http://www.jobprofiles.org/ jphowto.htm) if you have any problems.

Major Jobs Web Sites at Careers.org

http://www.careers.org/topic/01_jobs_ 10.html

This page at the Careers.org Web site has links for more than 40 of the Web's major job-related Web sites. While you're there, check out the numerous links to additional information.

Monster Jobs

http://www.monster.com

Monster.com is one of the largest, and probably best known, job resource sites on the Internet. It's really one-stop shopping for almost any job-related subject that you can imagine: Find a new job, network, update your resume, improve your skills, plan a job change or relocation, and so much more! Of special interest are the Monster: Cool Careers (http://change.monster.com/archives/ coolcareers) and the Monster: Job Profiles (http://jobprofiles.monster.com) sections, where you can read about some really neat careers. The short profiles also include links to additional information. The Monster: Career Advice section (http://content.monster.com) has resume and interviewing advice, message boards where you can network, relocation tools and advice, and more.

Occupational Outlook Handbook

http://www.bls.gov/oco

Published by the U.S. Department of Labor's Bureau of Labor Statistics, the Occupational Outlook Handbook *(sometimes referred to as the* OOH*) is the premiere source of career information. The book is updated every two years, so you can be assured that the information you are using to help make your decisions is current. The online version is very easy to use; you can search for a specific occupation, browse though a group of related occupations, or look through an alphabetical listing of all the jobs included in the volume. Each of the entries will highlight the general nature of the job, working conditions, training and other qualifications, job outlook, average earning, related occupations, and sources of additional information. Each entry covers several pages and is a terrific source to get some great information about a huge variety of jobs.*

The Riley Guide: Employment Opportunities and Job Resources on the Internet

http://www.rileyguide.com

The Riley Guide is an amazing collection of job and career resources. Unless you're looking for something specific, one of the best ways to maneuver around the site is with the A-to-Z Index. You can find everything from links to careers in enology to information about researching companies and employers. The Riley Guide is a great place to find just about anything you're looking for, and probably lots of things you never dreamed you wanted to know! But be forewarned—it's easy to get lost in the A-to-Z Index, because it's filled with so many interesting things.

USA TODAY Career Focus

http://www.usatoday.com/careers/dream/ dreamarc.htm

USA TODAY *offers their "dream job" series on this Web site. In these interview profiles, people discuss how they got their dream job, what they enjoy the most about it, describe an average day, their education backgrounds, sacrifices they had to make for their jobs, and more. They also share words of advice for anyone hoping to follow in their footsteps. Most of the articles also feature links where you can find more information. The USATODAY.com Job Center (http://www.usatoday.com/money/jobcenter/front.htm) also has links to lots of resources and additional information.*

CAREER TESTS AND INVENTORIES

If you have no idea what career is right for you, there are many resources available online that you can use to categorize your interests and steer you in the right direction. While some of the assessments charge a fee, many others are free. You can locate more tests and inventories by searching for the keywords career tests, career inventories, or personality inventories. Some of the most popular assessments available online are:

Campbell Interest and Skill Survey (CISS)
http://www.usnews.com/usnews/edu/careers/ccciss.htm

Career Explorer
http://careerexplorer.net/aptitude.asp

Career Focus 2000 Interest Inventory
http://www.iccweb.com/careerfocus

The Career Interests Game
http://career.missouri.edu/students/explore/thecareerinterestsgame.php

The Career Key
http://www.careerkey.org

Career Maze
http://www.careermaze.com/home.asp?licensee=CareerMaze

Career Tests at CareerPlanner.com
http://www.careerplanner.com

CAREERLINK Inventory
http://www.mpc.edu/cl/cl.htm

FOCUS
http://www.focuscareer.com

Keirsey Temperament Test
http://www.keirsey.com

Motivational Appraisal of Personal Potential (MAPP)
http://www.assessment.com

Myers-Briggs Personality Type
http://www.personalitypathways.com/type_inventory.html

Skills Profiler
http://www.acinet.org/acinet/skills_home.asp

Princeton Review Career Quiz
http://www.princetonreview.com/cte/quiz/default.asp

APPENDIX C: FILM SCHOOLS

American Film Institute
2021 North Western Avenue
Los Angeles, CA 90027-1657
(323) 856-7600
http://www.afi.com

Brooklyn College–Department of Film
2900 Bedford Avenue
201 West End Building (WEB)
Brooklyn, NY 11210-2889
(718) 951-5664
film@brooklyn.cuny.edu
http://depthome.brooklyn.cuny.edu/film/
frames/index.html

Columbia University School of the Arts
Columbia University
305 Dodge Hall, Mail Code 1808
2960 Broadway
New York, NY 10027
(212) 854-2875
film@columbia.edu
http://arts.columbia.edu/index.
cfm?fuseaction=film_div.main

Duke University
Program in Film/Video/Digital
104 Crowell Hall
Box 90671
Durham, NC 27708-0671
(919) 660-3030
info@duke.edu/web/film
http://www.duke.edu/web/film

Hollywood Film Institute
PO Box 481252
Los Angeles, CA 90048
(310) 399-6699
info@webfilmschool.com
http://www.hollywoodu.com

London International Film School
24 Shelton Street
London WC2H 9UB
United Kingdom
info@lfs.org.uk
+44 (0) 20 7836 9642
http://www.lifs.org.uk

The Los Angeles Film School
6363 Sunset Boulevard, Suite 500
Los Angeles, CA 90028
(877) 952-3456
info@lafilm.com
http://www.lafilm.com/index.cfm/Home

San Francisco State
University—Cinema Department
1600 Holloway Avenue
San Francisco, CA 94132
(415) 338-1629
cinedept@sfsu.edu
http://www.cinema.sfsu.edu

UCLA School of Theater,
Film, and Television
102 East Melnitz Hall
Box 951622
Los Angeles, CA 90095
(310) 825-5761
info@tft.ucla.edu
http://www.filmtv.ucla.edu

READ MORE ABOUT IT

The following sources and books may help you learn more about entertainment careers.

GENERAL CAREERS

Blumenthal, Howard J., and Oliver R. Goodenough. *This Business of Television.* New York: Billboard Books, 1991.

Culbreath, Alice N., and Saundra K. Neal. *Testing the Waters: A Teen's Guide to Career Exploration.* New York: JRC Consulting, 1999.

Farr, Michael, LaVerne L. Ludden, and Laurence Shatkin. *200 Best Jobs for College Graduates.* Indianapolis, Ind.: Jist Publishing, 2003.

Fitzsimmons, April. *Breaking & Entering: A Career Guide About Landing Your First Job in Film Production...and Living to Tell About It!* Hollywood: Lone Eagle Publishing Company, 1997.

Fogg, Neeta, Paul Harrington, and Thomas Harrington. *College Majors Handbook with Real Career Paths and Payoffs: The Actual Jobs, Earnings, and Trends for Graduates of 60 College Majors.* Indianapolis, Ind.: Jist Publishing, 2004.

Hiam, Alex, and Susan Angle. *Adventure Careers: Your Guide to Exciting Jobs, Uncommon Occupations and Extraordinary Experiences.* 2nd ed.. Franklin Lakes, N.J.: Career Press, 1995.

Jakubiak, Joyce, ed. *Specialty Occupational Outlook: Trade and Technical.* Detroit: Gale Research, Inc., 1996.

Krannich, Ronald L., and Caryl Rae Krannich. *The Best Jobs for the 1990s and into the 21st Century.* Manassas Park, Va.: Impact Publications, 1995.

Levy, Frederick. *Hollywood 101, The Film Industry How to Succeed in Hollywood Without Connections.* Riverside, Calif.: Renaissance Books, 2000.

Mannion, James. *The Everything Alternative Careers Book: Leave the Office Behind and Embark on a New Adventure.* Boston: Adams, 2004.

Resnik, Gail, and Scott Trost. *All You Need to Know About the Movie and TV Business.* New York: Fireside, 1996.

U.S. Bureau of Labor Statistics. *Occupational Outlook Handbook, 2004-05.* Available online at http://careerplanning.about.com/gi/dynamic/offsite.htm?site=http%3A%2F%2Fwww.bls.gov%2Foco%2F.

ANIMAL WRANGLER

Applebaum, Steven. *ABC Practical Guide to Dog Training.* Hoboken, N.J.: Howell Book House, 2003.

Katz, Adam. *Secrets of a Professional Dog Trainer.* Available online at http://www.dogproblems.com/secretsbook.htm.

Wilde, Nicole. *So You Want To Be A Dog Trainer.* Santa Clarita, Calif.: Phantom Publishing, 2001.

Wilde, Nicole. *It's Not the Dogs, It's the People! A Dog Trainer's Guide to Training Humans.* Santa Clarita, Calif.: Phantom Publishing, 2003.

BEST BOY

Block, Bruce. *The Visual Story: Seeing the Structure of Film, TV and New Media.* Burlington, Mass.: Focal Press, 2001.

Katz, Steven. *Film Directing: Shot by Shot: Visualizing from Concept to Screen.* Studio City, Calif.: Michael Wiese Productions, 1991.

Mascelli, Joseph V. *The Five C's of Cinematography: Motion Picture Filming Techniques.* Los Angeles: Silman-James Press, 1998.

Taub, Eric. *Gaffers, Grips and Best Boys: From Producer-Director to Gaffer and Computer Special Effects Creator, a Behind-the-Scenes Look at Who Does What in the Making of a Motion Picture.* New York: St. Martin's Griffin, 1995.

BOOM OPERATOR

Duncan, Ben. *The Live Sound Manual: Getting Great Sound at Every Gig.* San Francisco: Backbeat Books, 2002.

Mills-Huber, David, and Philip Williams. *Professional Microphone Techniques.* Stamford, Conn.: Artistpro, a division of Thomson Learning, Inc., 1999.

White, Paul. *Basic Live Sound.* London: Sanctuary Publishing, Ltd., 2000.

White, Paul. Basic *Microphones.* London: Sanctuary Publishing, Ltd., 2000.

Young, Clive. *Crank It Up: Live Sound Secrets of the Top Tour Engineers.* San Francisco: Backbeat Books, 2004.

CAMERA OPERATOR

Ascher, Steven, and Edward Pincus. *The Filmmaker's Handbook: A Compre-hensive Guide for the Digital Age.* New York: Plume Books, 1999.

Carlson, Sylvia E. *The Professional Cameraman's Handbook.* Burlington, Mass.: Focal Press, 1993.

Landau, Camille, and Tiara White. *What They Don't Teach You At Film School: 161 Strategies to Making Your Own Movie No Matter What.* New York: Hyperion, 2000.

Mascelli, Joseph V. *The Five C's of Cinematography: Motion Picture Filming Techniques.* Los Angeles: Silman-James Press, 1998.

Newton, Dale. *Digital Filmmaking 101: An Essential Guide to Producing Low Budget Movies.* Studio City, Calif.: Michael Wiese Productions, 2001.

Rodriguez, Robert. *Rebel Without a Crew: Or How a 23-Year-Old Filmmaker With $7,000 Became a Hollywood Player.* New York: Plume Books, 1996.

Stern, Bret. *How to Shoot a Feature Film for Under $10,000 (And Not Go to Jail).* New York: HarperResource, 2002.

Vineyard, Jeremy. *Setting Up Your Shots: Great Camera Moves Every Filmmaker Should Know.* Studio City, Calif.: Michael Wiese Productions, 2000.

CASTING DIRECTOR

Hennessey, Debbie, and Kevin Oaks. *Agents, Managers and Casting Directors 411.* Los Angeles: LA 411 Publishing Company, 2001.

Howard, Ginger. *Casting Directors' Secrets.* New York: Allworth Press, 2000.

Hurtes, Hetty Lynn. *The Back Stage Guide to Casting Directors: Who They Are, How They Work, and What They Look* for in Actors. New York: Back Stage Books, 1992.

CELEBRITY ASSISTANT

Havens, John C. *Fabjob Guide to Become a Celebrity Personal Assistant.* Available online at http://www.fabjob.com/celebrity.asp.

Howard, Heather. *Chore Whore: Adventures of a Celebrity Personal Assistant.* New York: HarperCollins Publisher, 2005.

Longson, Sally. *Getting a Top Job as a Personal Assistant.* London: Kogan Page, 2002.

Muhammad, Dionne M. *Beyond The Red Carpet: Keys To Becoming A Successful Personal Assistant.* Bloomington, Ind.: Authorhouse, 2004.

Robinson, Bill, and Ceridwen Morris. *It's All Your Fault: How to Make It as a Hollywood Assistant.* New York: Fireside, 2001.

CELEBRITY PHOTOGRAPHER

Eisler, Colin, et al. *Irving Penn, A Career in Photography.* New York: Bulfinch Press, 1997.

Frost, Lee. *Teach Yourself Photography.* New York: McGraw-Hill, 2004.

Grimm, Tom, and Michele Grimm. *The Basic Book of Photography,* 5th Edition. New York: Plume Books, 2003.

Hambourg, Maria Morris, et al. *Richard Avedon Portraits.* New York: Harry N. Abrams, 2002.

Hart, John. *50 Portrait Lighting Techniques for Pictures that Sell.* New York: Watson Guptill Publications, Inc. 1995.

Hunter, Fil, and Paul Fuqua. *Light: Science and Magic: An Introduction to Photographic Lighting.* Burlington, Mass.: Elsevier Science & Technology Books, 1997.

McCartney, Susan. *Mastering the Basics of Photography.* New York: Watson-Guptill Publications, 2001.

Sherman, Cindy, and Peter Galassi. *Cindy Sherman: Film Stills.* New York: Museum of Modern Art, 2003.

CLOWN

Feder, Happy Jack. *Clown Skits for Everyone: Everything You Need to Know to Become a Performing Clown.* Colorado Springs, Colo.: Meriwether Publishing Ltd., 1991.

Fife, Bruce. *The Birthday Party Business: How to Make a Living As a Children's Entertainer.* Colorado Springs, Colo.: Piccadilly Books, 1998.

Fife, Bruce. *Creative Clowning.* Colorado Springs, Colo.: Piccadilly Books, 1992.

Gaskin, Carol. *A Day in the Life of a Circus Clown.* Mahwah, N.J.: Troll Communications LLC., 1987.

Pipkin, Turk. *Be a Clown!: The Complete Guide to Instant Clowning.* New York: Workman Publishing Company, 1989.

Sminkey, Donald C. *Handbook for the Magical Party Clown.* Bowie, Md.: Clown Capers, 1991.

COMEDIAN

Allen, Steve and Jane Wollman. *How to Be Funny: Discovering the Comic You.* Essex, England: Prometheus Books, 1998.

Carter, Judy. *The Comedy Bible: From Stand-up to Sitcom—The Comedy Writer's Ultimate "How To" Guide.* New York: Fireside, 2001.

———. *Stand-Up Comedy: The Book.* New York: Dell, 1989.

Helitzer, Melvin. *Comedy Writing Secrets.* Cincinnatti: Writer's Digest Books, 1992.

Kachuba, John B. *How to Write Funny: Add Humor to Every Kind of Writing.* Cincinnati: Writer's Digest Books, 2001.

Macks, Jon. *How to Be Funny.* New York: Simon & Schuster, 2003.

Mendrinos, James. *Complete Idiot's Guide to Comedy Writing.* New York: Alpha, 2004.

Menzel-Gerrie, Sharon. *Careers in Comedy.* New York: Rosen Publishing Group, 1993.

Perret, Gene. *Comedy Writing Step by Step.* London: Samuel French, 1990.

Schreiber, Brad. *What are You Laughing At?: How to Write Funny Screenplays, Stories, and More.* Studio City, Calif.: Michael Wiese Productions, 2003.

Schwensen, Dave. *How to Be a Working Comic: An Insider's Guide to a Career in Stand-Up Comedy.* New York: Watson-Guptill Publications, 1998.

Vorhaus, John. *The Comic Toolbox: How to Be Funny Even If You're Not.* Los Angeles: Silman-James Press, 1994.

White, Karyn Ruth, and Jay Arthur. *Your Seventh Sense: How to Think Like a Comedian.* Denver: Lifestar Publishing, 2004.

DIRECTOR OF PHOTOGRAPHY

Ettedgui, Peter. *Cinematography.* Burlington, Mass.: Focal Press, 1999.

Rodriguez, Robert. *Rebel Without a Crew: Or How a 23-Year-Old Filmmaker With $7,000 Became a Hollywood Player.* New York: Plume Books, 1996.

Selakovich, Dan. *Killer Camera Rigs That You Can Build: How to Build Your Own Camera Cranes, Car Mounts, Stabilizers, Dollies, and More.* Los Angeles: Angel Dog Entertainment, 2003.

DOCUMENTARY FILMMAKER

Barbash, Illisa, and Lucien Taylor. *Cross-Cultural Filmmaking: A Handbook for Making Documentary and Ethnographic Films and Videos.* Berkeley: University of California Press, 1997.

Bruzzi, Stella. *New Documentary: A Critical Introduction.* Oxford, U.K.: Routledge, 2000.

Nichols, Bill. *Introduction to Documentary.* Bloomington, Ind.: Indiana University Press, 2001.

Rodriguez, Robert. *Rebel Without a Crew: Or How a 23-Year-Old Filmmaker With $7,000 Became a Hollywood Player.* New York: Plume Books, 1996.

FIGHT CHOREOGRAPHER

Clements, John. *Renaissance Swordsmanship: The Illustrated Book Of Rapiers And Cut And Thrust Swords And Their Use.* Boulder, CO: Paladin Press, 1997.

Ducklin, Keith. *Sword Fighting: A Manual for Actors and Directors.* New York: Applause Books, 2001.

Girard, Dale. *Actors on Guard: A Practical Guide for the Use of the Rapier and Dagger for Stage and Screen.* Oxford, U.K.: Routledge, 1996.

Kreng, John. *Fight Choreography: The Art of Non-Verbal Dialog.* Boston: Muska & Lipman/Premier, 2005.

Lane, Richard. *Swashbuckling: A Step-by-Step Guide to the Art of Stage Combat and Theatrical Swordplay.* New York: Limelight Editions, 2004.

Witney, William. *In a Door, Into a Fight, Out a Door, Into a Chase: Moviemak-*

ing Remembered by the Guy at the Door. Jefferson, N.C.: McFarland & Company, 1995.

FOCUS PULLER
Goldman, Lewis. *Lights, Camera, Action! Behind the Scenes Making Movies.* New York: Harry N. Abrams, 1986.

Patterson, Freeman. *Photography And The Art Of Seeing: A Visual Perception Workshop For Film And Digital Photography.* Toronto: Key Porter Books, 2004.

Vineyard, Jeremy. *Setting Up Your Shots: Great Camera Moves Every Filmmaker Should Know.* Studio City, Calif.: Michael Wiese Productions, 2000.

LOCATION SCOUT
Gordon, William A. *Shot on This Site: A Traveler's Guide to the Places and Locations Used to Film Famous Movies and TV Shows.* Secaucus, N.J.: Carol Publishing Corporation, 1995.

Katz, Chuck. *Manhattan on Film: Walking Tours of Hollywood's Fabled Front Lot.* New York: Limelight Editions, 2004.

Reeves, Tony. *The Worldwide Guide to Movie Locations.* Chicago: Chicago Review Press, 2001.

Zoomer Guides. *Zoomer Guide to NYC's Most Famous T.V. and Movie Locations.* San Diego: Merchant Publishing, 2003.

MOTIVATIONAL SPEAKER
Axtell, Roger. *Do's and Taboos of Public Speaking: How to Get Those Butterflies Flying in Formation.* Hoboken, N.J.: John Wiley & Sons, 1992.

Jeary, Tony, J.E. Fishman and Kim Dower. *Life Is a Series of Presentations: 8 Ways to Punch Up Your People Skills at Work, at Home, Anytime, Anywhere.* New York: Simon & Schuster Adult Publishing Group, 2003.

Walters, Lilly, and Anita Roddick. *Secrets of Superstar Speakers: Wisdom from the Greatest Motivators of Our Time.* New York: The McGraw-Hill Companies, 2000.

Wilder, Lilyan. *7 Steps to Fearless Speaking.* Hoboken, N.J.: John Wiley & Sons, 1999.

OPERA SINGER
Fleming, Renee. *The Inner Voice: The Making of a Singer.* New York: Viking Books, 2004.

Griffiths, Paul. *When Divas Confess: Master Opera Singers in Their Leading Roles.* New York: Universe Publishing, 1999.

Matheopoulos, Helena. *Diva: The New Generation: The Sopranos and Mezzos of the Decade Discuss Their Roles.* Boston: Northeastern University Press, 1998.

———. *Divo: Great Tenors, Baritones and Basses Discuss Their Roles.* New York: HarperCollins, 1986.

Opera News. New York: The Metropolitan Opera Guild. Also available online at http://www.metoperafamily.org/operanews/index.aspx.

Story, Rosalyn M. *And So I Sing: African-American Divas of Opera and Concert.* New York: Warner Books, 1990.

ORCHESTRA CONDUCTOR
Carlinsky, Dan, and Ed Goodgold. *The Armchair Conductor: How to Lead*

a Symphony Orchestra in the Privacy of Your Own Home. New York: Dell, 1991.

Dennis, Paulina. *The Story of an American Orchestra Conductor.* Akron, Ohio: Writers Club Press, 2001.

Van Horn, James. *The Community Orchestra: A Handbook for Conductors, Managers, and Boards.* Westport, Conn.: Greenwood Press, 1979.

POSTPRODUCTION SUPERVISOR

Case, Dominic. *Film Technology in Post Production.* 2nd edition. Burlington, Mass.: Focal Press, 2001.

Clark, Barbara. *Guide to Postproduction for TV and Film: Managing the Process.* 2nd edition. Burlington, Mass.: Focal Press, 2002.

Rogers, Lynne. *Working in Show Business: Behind-The-Scenes Careers in Theater, Film, and Television.* New York: Back Stage Books, 1998.

Wyatt, Hilary, and Tim Amyes. *Audio Post Production for Television and Film: An Introduction to Technology and Techniques.* Burlington, Mass.: Focal Press, 2004.

PRODUCT PLACEMENT SPECIALIST

Cappo, Joe. *The Future of Advertising: New Media, New Clients, New Consumers in the Post-Television Age.* New York: McGraw-Hill, 2003.

Clark, Kevin. *Brandscendence: Three Essential Elements of Enduring Brands.* Chicago: Dearborn Trade, 2004.

Galician, Mary-Lou. *Handbook of Product Placement in the Mass Media: New Strategies in Marketing Theory, Prac-* *tice, Trends, and Ethics.* New York: Better Business Books, 2004.

Segrave, Kerry. *Product Placement in Hollywood Films: A History.* Jefferson, N.C.: McFarland & Company, 2004.

PROP MASTER

Gordon, Sandra. *Action!: Establishing Your Career in Film and Television Production.* New York: Applause Books, 2002.

Resnik, Gail. *All You Need to Know About the Movie and TV Business.* 5th Edition. New York: Fireside, 1996.

Rogers, Lynne. *Working in Show Business: Behind-The-Scenes Careers in Theater, Film, and Television.* New York: Back Stage Books, 1998.

PUPPETEER

Abrams, Steve. *American Puppetry: Collections, History and Performance.* Jefferson, N.C.: McFarland & Company, 2004.

Bell, John. *Puppets, Masks and Performing Objects.* Cambridge, Mass.: MIT Press, 2001.

Blumenthal, Eileen. *Puppetry: A World History.* New York: Harry N. Abrams, 2005.

Currell, David. *Puppets and Puppet Theater.* London: Crowood Press, 1999.

Latshaw, George. *The Complete Book of Puppetry.* Dover Publications, 2000.

SCENE CONSTRUCTION EXPERT

Blurton, John. *Scenery: Draughting and Construction for Theatres, Museums, Exhibitions and Trade Shows.* Oxford: Routledge, 2001.

Gillette, J. Michael. *Theatrical Design and Production: An Introduction to Scene Design and Construction, Lighting, Sound, Costume, and Makeup.* New York: McGraw-Hill, 1999.

Ionazzi, Daniel A. *The Stagecraft Handbook.* Cincinnati: Betterway Books, 1996.

Lounsbury, Warren C. *Theatre Backstage from A to Z.* Seattle: University of Washington Press, 1999.

Miller, James Hull. *Small Stage Sets on Tour: A Practical Guide to Portable Stage Sets.* Colorado Springs, Colo.: Meriwether Publishing, Ltd, 1987.

SCREENWRITER

de Abreu, Carlos. *Opening the Doors to Hollywood: How to Sell Your Idea, Story, Screenplay, Manuscript.* New York: Three Rivers Press, 1997.

Atchity, Kenneth, and Chi-Li Wong. *Writing Treatments That Sell: How to Create and Market Your Story Ideas to the Motion Picture and TV Industry.* 2nd ed. New York: Owl Books, 2003.

DiMaggio, Madeline. *How to Write For Television.* New York: Fireside, 1990.

Flinn, Denny Martin. *How Not to Write a Screenplay: 101 Common Mistakes Most Screenwriters Make.* Hollywood: Lone Eagle Publishing Company, 1999.

Halperin, Michael. *Writing the Killer Treatment: Selling Your Story Without a Script.* Studio City, Calif.: Michael Wiese Productions, 2002.

Iglesias, Karl. *The 101 Habits of Highly Successful Screenwriters: Insider's Secrets from Hollywood's Top Writers.* Boston: Adams Media Corporation, 2001.

Keane, Christopher. *How to Write a Selling Screenplay.* New York: Broadway, 1998.

Lerch, Jennifer. *500 Ways to Beat the Hollywood Script Reader: Writing the Screenplay the Reader Will Recommend.* New York: Fireside, 1999.

McGrath, Declan, and Felim MacDermott. *Screenwriting.* Burlington, Mass.: Focal Press, 2003.

McKee, Robert. *Story: Substance, Structure, Style and The Principles of Screenwriting.* New York: Regan Books, 1997.

Press, Skip. *Complete Idiot's Guide to Screenwriting.* New York: Alpha Books, 2000.

Schellhardt, Laura, and John Logan. *Screenwriting for Dummies.* Hoboken, N.J.: Dummies/Wiley, 2003.

Schreiber, Brad. *What are You Laughing at?: How to Write Funny Screenplays, Stories, and More.* Studio City, Calif.: Michael Wiese Productions, 2003.

Seger, Linda. *Making a Good Script Great.* 2nd edition. London: Samuel French Trade, 1987.

Stoller, Bryan Michael. *Filmmaking for Dummies.* Hoboken, N.J.: Dummies/Wiley, 2003.

Trottier, David. *The Screenwriter's Bible: A Complete Guide to Writing, Formatting, and Selling Your Script.* Los Angeles: Silman-James Press, 1998.

Whiteside, Rich. *The Screenwriting Life: The Dream, the Job, and the Reality.* New York: Berkley Publishing Group, 1998.

SET MEDIC

Hafen, Brent Q., Keith J. Karren, and Joseph J. Mistovich. *Prehospital Emergency Care.* 7th ed. Paramus, N.J.: Prentice Hall, 2003.

Limmer, Daniel. *Emergency Care.* 9th Edition. Paramus, N.J.: Prentice Hall, 2000.

SOUND MIXER

Katz, Bob. *Mastering Audio: the Art and the Science*. Burlington, Mass.: Focal Press, 2002.

Moscal, Tony. *The Basics of Sound and Sound Systems*. Milwaulkee, Wisc.: Hal Leonard Corporation, 1999.

Owsinski, Bobby. *The Mixing Engineer's Handbook*. Stamford, Conn.: Artistpro, a division of Thomson Learning, Inc., 1999.

White, Paul. *Basic Mixing Techniques*. London: Sanctuary Publishing, Ltd., 2000.

SPECIAL EFFECTS TECHNICIAN

McCarthy, Roberts. *Secrets of Hollywood Special Effects*. Burlington, Mass.: Focal Press, 1992.

Pinteau, Pascal, and Laurel Hirsch. *Special Effects: An Oral History—Interviews with 37 Masters Spanning 100 Years*. New York: Harry N. Abrams, 2005.

Rickitt, Richard. *Special Effects: The History and Techniques*. New York: Watson-Guptill Publications, 2000.

Vinther, Janus. *Special Effects Makeup*. New York: Routledge, 2003.

STORYBOARD ARTIST

Begleiter, Marcie. *From Word to Image: Storyboarding and the Filmmaking Process*. Studio City, Calif.: Michael Wiese Productions, 2001.

Bluth, Don. *Don Bluth's Art of Storyboard*. Milwaukie, Ore.: DH Press, 2004.

Canemaker, John. *Paper Dreams: The Art And Artists Of Disney Storyboards*. Burbank: Disney Editions, 1999.

Fraioli, James. *Storyboarding 101: A Crash Course in Professional Storyboarding*. Studio City, Calif.: Michael Wiese Productions, 2000.

Hart, John. *The Art of the Storyboard: Storyboarding for Film, TV, and Animation*. Burlington, Mass.: Focal Press, 1998.

Simon, Mark. *Storyboards: Motion in Art*, Second Edition. Burlington, Mass.: Focal Press, 2000.

STUDIO TEACHER

Brock Harris. *How to Become a Studio Teacher*. Los Angeles: Brock Harris, 2002.

Feirsen, Robert. *How to Get the Teaching Job You Want: The Complete Guide for College Graduates, Teachers Changing Schools, Returning Teachers and Career Changers*. New York: Stylus Pub LLC, 2004.

STUNT PERFORMER

Asbett, Mark, and Mark Aisbett. *So You Wanna Be a Stuntman: The Official Stuntman's Guidebook*. British Columbia, Vancouver: Lifedrivers Inc., 1999.

Bucklin, Jack. *Stuntman: A Freelancer's Guide To Learning The Craft And Landing The Jobs*. Falls Church, Va.: Paladin Press, 1992.

Emmens, Carol A. *Stunt Work and Stunt People*. London: Franklin Watts, 1982.

Kent, Peter Harris. *Stand or Fall: An Autobiography of a Stuntman*. Bloomington, Ind.: Authorhouse, 2001.

Weld, John. *Fly Away Home: Memoirs of a Hollywood Stuntman*. Palo Alto, Calif.: Mission Publishing Company, 1991.

VENTRILOQUIST

Engler, Larry, and Carol Fijan. *Making Puppets Come Alive: How to Learn and*

Teach Hand Puppetry. Mineola, N.Y.: Dover Publications, 1997.

King, Kolby. *Ventriloquism Made Easy*. Mineola, N.Y.: Dover Publications, 1997.

VOICE-OVER ARTIST

Alburger, James. *The Art of Voice Acting: The Craft and Business of Performing for Voice-Over*. 2nd ed. Burlington, Mass.: Focal Press, 2002.

Apple, Teri. *Making Money in Voice-Overs: Winning Strategies To A Successful Career In Commercials, Cartoons and Radio*. Hollywood: Lone Eagle Publishing Company, 1999.

Blu, Susan. *Word of Mouth: A Guide to Commercial Voice-Over Excellence*. Beverly Hills, Calif.: Pomegranate Press, 1992.

Clark, Elaine. *There's Money Where Your Mouth Is: An Insider's Guide to a Career in Voice-Overs*. 2nd ed. New York: Back Stage Books, 2000.

WARDROBE ASSISTANT

Gordon, Sandra. *Action!: Establishing Your Career in Film and Television Production*. New York: Applause Books, 2002.

Resnik, Gail. *All You Need to Know About the Movie and TV Business*. 5th edition. New York: Fireside, 1996.

Rogers, Lynne. *Working in Show Business: Behind-The-Scenes Careers in Theater, Film, and Television*. New York: Back Stage Books, 1998.

INDEX

Page numbers in **bold** indicate main entries.